# NEXT GENERATION SUPPLY CHAINS

## THE GUIDE FOR BUSINESS LEADERS

Michel FENDER

Copyright © 2020 Michel Fender

All rights reserved. No part of this publication may be reproduced or transmitted in any form or by any means, electronic or mechanical including photocopying, recording or any information storage or retrieval system, without prior permission in writing from the publishers.

The right of Michel Fender to be identified as the author of this work has been asserted by him in accordance with the Copyright, Designs and Patents Act 1988

First published in the United Kingdom in 2020 by
The Choir Press

ISBN 978-1-78963-115-9

# Contents

| | |
|---|---|
| Acknowledgements | v |
| Introduction | vii |
| | |
| Part A: Use supply chain management (SCM) to generate business value | 1 |
| | |
| Part A Introduction. What are we talking about? Some key definitions | 3 |
| 1   The five-parameter value equation of supply chain | 15 |
|     Company Testimony: Essilor International | 20 |
| 2   Boost your top line by developing customer satisfaction | 25 |
|     Testimony: 3M | 30 |
| 3   Minimise the cost-to-serve | 35 |
|     Company testimony: Trinseo | 40 |
| 4   Generate cash | 45 |
| 5   Maximise the operational and financial value of your assets | 52 |
|     Testimony: Saint-Gobain Glass | 60 |
| 6   Focus on sustainable and resilient supply chains | 65 |
| 7   Clarify your value proposition based on the first paradigm of SCM: trade-off | 70 |
|     Testimony: Nespresso | 75 |
| 8   Financialise your supply chain management to generate value | 81 |
|     Testimony: Wall Street Influencer | 85 |

## Contents

Part B: Design and animate the right supply chain (SC) models to create a competitive advantage — 89

Part B Introduction. Fundamental analytics for agile and resilient supply chains — 91

9  Innovate and invest in the right digital supply chain operating system — 100
   Testimony: Aera Technology — 109

10 Create a competitive advantage based on the second paradigm of SCM: the fair value — 114
   Testimony: OCP — 120

11 Control your supply chain performance — 127

12 Segment your SC models to support specific business strategies — 134
   Testimony: Andros — 145

13 Be agile and build One Team through IBP (Integrated Business Planning) — 150
   Testimony: CertainTeed — 158

14 Use SCM to transform your company — 164
   Company Testimony: Saint-Gobain Gypsum and Insulation — 176

Pre-conclusion: Apply SC mindset, concepts and tools to any type of organisation — 180
Testimony: Car.Software Organization by Volkswagen — 185

Conclusion — 187
Glossary — 189
Bibliography — 190

# Acknowledgements

Learning and sharing are key pillars of my mindset. The essence of cooperation within a network of multiple players in supply chain management has driven my professional life to develop a community of people involved in this field. My modest value-added is to animate a continuous journey between the real business life and innovative concepts, and then to formalise practices and methodologies.

This book is the outcome of this journey, combining three profiles of people:

- The professionals, who trust me to support the transformation of their business model by selecting the right topics to invest in. I never start working as a senior advisor with pre-packed solutions. I believe in the powerful attitude of co-building ideas and solutions, and supporting internal teams to successfully implement it. Among them, I particularly thank the top representatives of 3M, Aera Technology, Andros, CertainTeed, Essilor International, Nespresso, OCP, Saint-Gobain Construction, Saint-Gobain Glass, Trinseo, Volkswagen Car.Software Company, who have contributed to the credentials of this book.
- The participants essentially from Executive Masters and from custom programs at HEC Paris and Africa Business School (UM6P). I love turning around the mindset of those trainees from, in the best case, a sceptical perception to a convinced awareness of a fundamental topic to consider. I would like especially to mention the participants of TRIUM (HEC-LSE-NYU), who are respectful, strong challengers and who have been enabling me year after year to make significant progress in my thinking process to always better link supply chain to business value creation.
- My colleagues at Africa Business School (UM6P) and HEC Paris and from other institutions, especially in leadership, strategy, finance and marketing. Their insights are absolutely valuable and irreplaceable. Supply chain performance relies on a cross-functional perspective and leverages the strategy into operational excellence.

This book belongs to them and I hope it will stimulate newcomers to join this community of people who believe in the value of supply chain to make a better place to live.

# Introduction

Covid-19 has highlighted the critical role of supply chains. Unfortunately, this emphasis is the result of a major crisis and now more than ever, there is an underestimation of those roles and a clear confusion between supply chain, logistics and supply chain management. This book started being written in the second half of 2019. The lockdown enabled this author to complete and to enrich it. But to be honest, this crisis has not dramatically changed its content, and the fundamental messages were already embedded prior to Covid-19 and advocated for a new generation of supply chains.

Actually, leaders have been considering supply chain management (SCM) as a support activity to their business, which means supporting the value-added operations such as procurement, production, sales and marketing. As a consequence, leaders appreciate SCM as a cost-added activity, certainly useful but complex and too technical. The less they hear about it, for instance in terms of deliveries shutdown to customers, the better they feel. In other words, they mainly look at the SCM performance as a function avoiding issues and negative impacts on the business.

The reverse perspective of this book is to convince leaders to go beyond this historical status of SCM and to use it as business leverage in a positive way of value creation. SCM is the most appropriate leverage for operationalising the strategy and for creating a competitive advantage. SCM can be used not only to make a difference on the bottom line but on the growth. For sure, the development of the technical expertise of SCM is quite impressive, but it would be a mistake to leave it under the control of specialists and experts.

The main drivers supporting the statement of SCM as a value-added function are the following:

- The volatility and the uncertainty of the markets in volume and in diversity, the occurrence of less predictable major events and, therefore, the need for both agile and resilient supply chains.
- The fragmentation of the value chains, by players, by geographies, by distribution channels, implying a higher level of management complexity.
- The multiplicity of the supply chains based on local, global and hybrid models.
- The financial stakes within supply chains in terms of cost-to-serve, working capital and return on assets.

# Introduction

- The increasing stakes related to sustainable development.
- The opportunity to boost the current business models or to reinvent them through the 4.0 solutions.

This book starts with some definitions in order to avoid any further confusion, follows with a first part focusing on the types of value SCM can provide to the business with a close link to finance, and then covers in the second part a selection of SCM solutions that leaders should consider implementing in order to get the benefits of a supply chain approach driven by value creation.

To stimulate an active and time-boxed reading, each chapter is built around visual graphs drafting the key concepts and terminology, and focused explanations are provided for sharing the main ideas. Most chapters are illustrated by a testimony involving business and supply chain leaders from major companies. A synthetic take-away for business leaders and the key questions to address conclude each chapter. If your time is limited, you can focus on reading only the take-away and the key questions.

## PART A
# Use SCM to generate business value

## Part A Introduction

# What are we talking about? Some key definitions

## Key definition #1: Supply chain (SC)

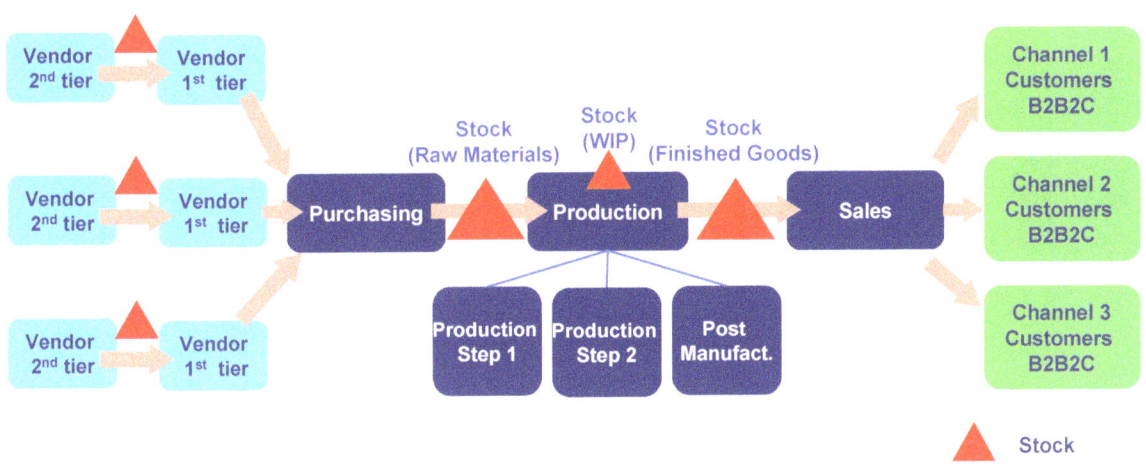

Diag. 1: The end-to-end supply chain

A supply chain consists of a multi-step chain of internal and external players. This is not an activity itself. Each industry (cosmetics, automotive, dry food, etc.) is characterised by a supply chain pattern:

- Fragmented versus integrated.
- Global versus local.

At each step, a specific value is generated. A **SC model** derives from a value chain model, which is designed through a strategic process based on the main following questions:

- Make vs buy: who does what? (Production and procurement strategies).
- How many players along the full chain and which margin to each? (Business strategy incl. tax optimisation).
- Single vs multiple sourcing (procurement sourcing).
- Which operations model? (Automation, process type, operations strategy).
- Which distribution channels? (Sales strategy).
- Which offer to customers? (Marketing strategy).

Complementary, the following questions enable afterwards to design an SC model:

- Which route-to-market? (How many steps to link our suppliers to our own facilities and then, from our facilities to our customers?)
- Where to locate the players? (Footprint strategy).
- What types of relationships with suppliers and customers? (Partnerships, collaboration, transactional).
- Which SC planning strategy (MTS vs MTO) and where to position the decoupling point (the point separating MTS upstream from MTO downstream), which enables to implement a late differentiation model? (See key definition #3).
- Where should inventories be and how large?

We generally distinguish:

- An internal supply chain made of the main functions taking part in the cycle from the sourcing of raw materials or traded goods to the delivery of the finished goods to the customers. In that case, the integration is horizontal among the functions. We talk about cross-functional collaboration between those players.
- The external supply chain embedding all the players taking part to the end-to-end supply chain from the last-tier vendor to the final consumer, including the recycling of used products. In that case, the integration is vertical among the players of the value chain.

Part A Introduction What are we talking about? Some key definitions

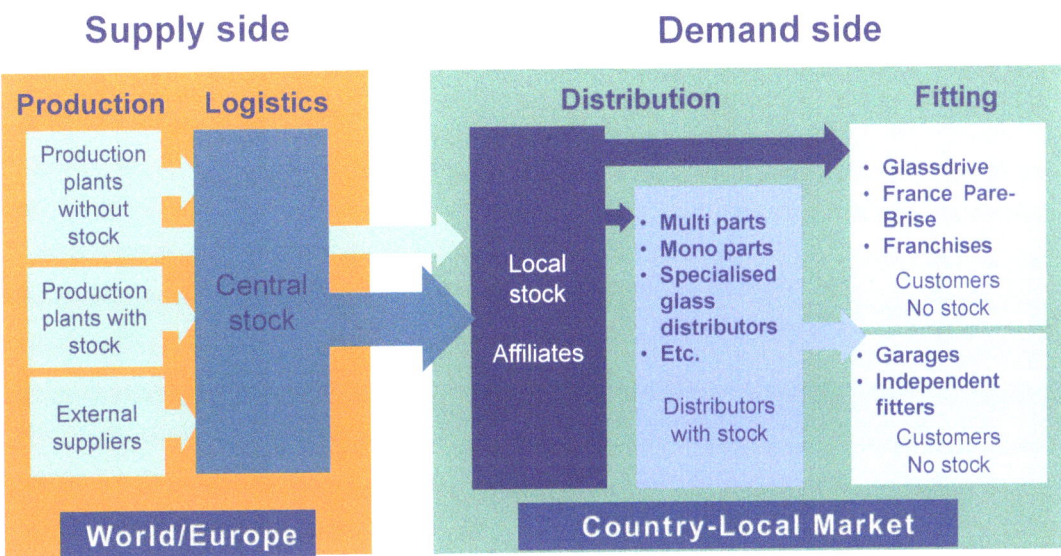

Diag.2: An example of a global–local supply chain

The above example shows an integrated global–local supply chain in the glass industry for the automotive replacement market:

- In the **supply side** of that supply chain, the floats produce raw glass on a continuous flow. The furnace is stopped for a cold maintenance only once a decade or even more. The raw glass can be coated and/or tempered. The floats supply factories producing windshields for the automotive market. Those factories are specialised in terms of their flexibility (batch size) and supply a central warehouse in Europe, which stores all the items for the country-based affiliates.
- In the **demand side**, those affiliates store the range of products appropriate for their market and distribute them either to the branded fitters or to different profiles of players such as car accessory distributors or specialised distributors, which resell to the fitting stations, are in contact with the final step of that supply chain as the car driver.

Interestingly, this example illustrates:

- The key notion of the supply side and the demand side of any supply chain.
- The fact that the supply side is global, which means the footprint of the factories is at the European and even at the world level (India and Thailand in that case), whereas

the demand side is definitely at the local level that means at the country level, characterised by specific market patterns and consumers habits.
- The differences between the sell-in (the volume of flows between players) and the sell-out (the volume of flows to the final customer). According to your position with the value chain, the sell-out is not necessarily under your control but is quite essential to enable you to forecast the market demand.

The application of the concept of supply chain leads to four generic patterns of supply chain, as shows the following table:

| Supply side | Demand side | Examples of business |
| --- | --- | --- |
| Local / regional | Local / regional | - Construction products<br>- Low value products<br>- Retail for local sourcing<br>- Fresh food<br>- Downstream part of lens industry |
| Local / regional | Global | - Automotive<br>- Aircraft<br>- Upstream part of lens industry |
| Global | Local / regional | - Luxury industry<br>- Dominant fashion model<br>- Retail for overseas sourcing<br>- High-value products |
| Global | Global | - Large corporations in FMCG such as cosmetics, chemicals, etc. |

Table 1: The four generic patterns of supply chain

We conclude this first definition by emphasising the fact that any player of a given value chain is part of a supply chain and potentially impacts its performance.

## Key definition #2: Logistics

Logistics covers operational execution (storage, handling, conveying, picking, packing, shipping, carrying, and delivery) done in logistics facilities such as distribution centres or hubs and supported by information systems such as warehouse management systems (WMS) and transportation management systems (TMS) and information technologies such as cloud. This is fundamentally resources-based activity that means it requires CAPEX. Innovations are quite important and both automation and digitalisation are trends, as show those pictures:

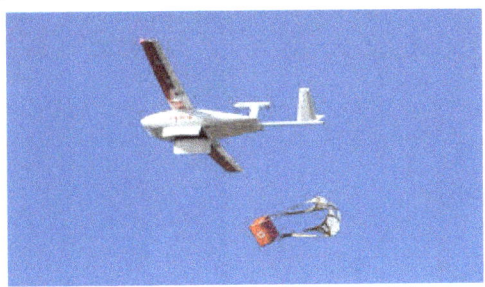

Diag.3: Examples of logistics solutions

Part A  Use SCM to generate business value

The top two pictures show a former manual picking model 'man-to-good' versus an automated model 'good-to-man' implemented by Amazon based on a Kiva system solution. The picking cost being the biggest part of the handling cost, its automation makes sense and enables as well to speed up the process and to respect the promise of a fast response to the shopper demand.

Innovation concerns the real estate as well, not only in terms of the development of XXL warehouses (>50,000 m² i.e. 540,000 sq ft) but the design and the implementation of multi-purpose urban buildings embedding housing, commercial, sport, shopping and even agricultural activities. The mid-left picture shows the last generation of warehouses in Japan, Prologis Park Zama 1 & Zama 2, located outside Tokyo. This five-story CASBEE-certified warehouse property has one of Japan's largest photovoltaic systems, setting the standard for sustainable industrial real estate in Japan.

In terms of transportation, trucking remains the dominant ground transportation means, but alternative solutions such as the deliveries of medicaments by drones in less-accessible regions like Africa have been developed.

As a conclusion of that second key definition, it is quite interesting to have a look at the patents developed by Amazon:

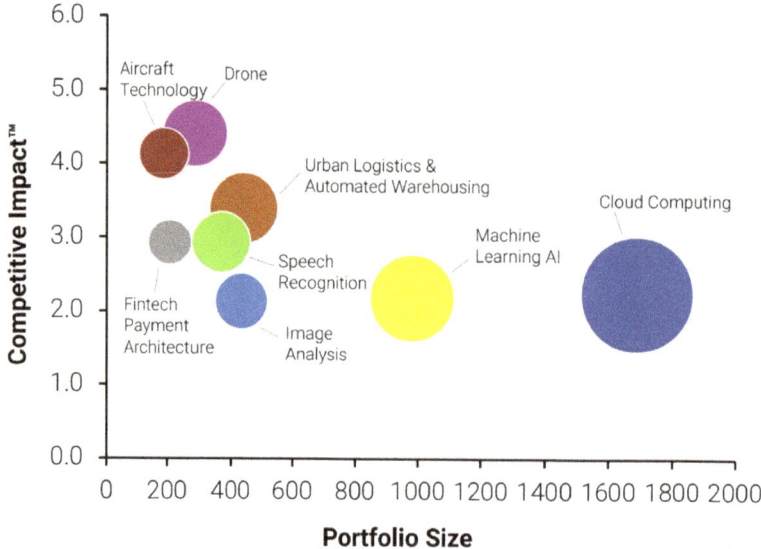

Active Portfolio of Amazon in selected technology fields. Data as on 4th July 2019.
Source: PatentSight Business Intelligence Platform www.patentsight.com

PatentSight database average of 1

Diag.4: Amazon patent mapping

This map shows the diversity of the domains of logistics and technologies covered by Amazon patents, their interdependency and the competitive impact they potentially provide, keeping in mind in the PatentSight database the average impact is 1.

## Key definition #3: Supply Chain Management (SCM)

Supply chain management is a monitoring process involving multiple players performing activities within a given supply chain and generating value to their clients. The following diagram shows the main components of SCM:

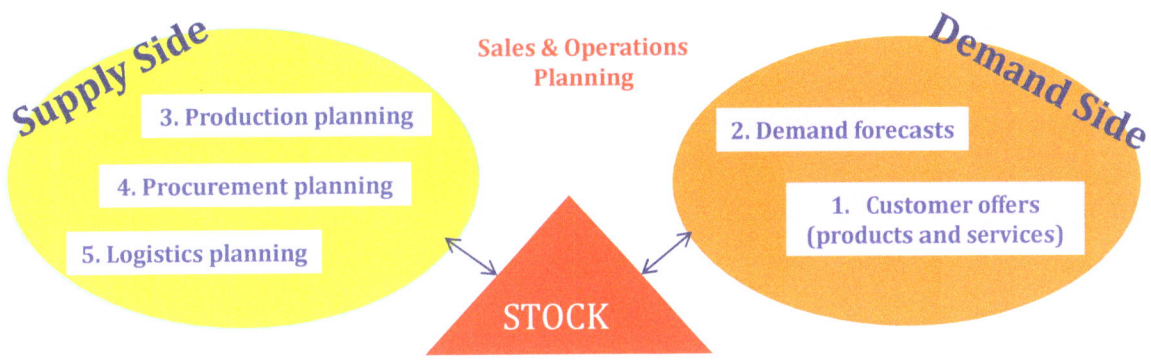

Diag.5: The supply chain management processes

This monitoring starts fundamentally with the formalisation of the customers offers in terms of both products and services, which can be formalised either through service charters or through service level agreements (SLA) for the key accounts, which can be segmented by customers, regions or channels. The second activity of SCM related to the demand side of the supply chain is the demand plan. Then, based on that demand plan, the supply side consists of three planning activities: production, procurement and logistics resources. The reconciliation of both sides is done by the major backbone of SCM called S&OP (Sales and Operations Planning) or even IBP (Integrated Business Planning), as we will see in Chapter 13. Stock management fully belongs to SCM as a key part of this reconciliation process.

We can consider SCM as a tactical process done on a monthly frequency with an eighteen-month horizon.

As we see with the value model definition in Chapter 14, SCM can be considered as the perfect leverage to link strategic ambition with operational excellence.

This is the right place to introduce the fundamental notion of **supply chain planning strategies** as displayed in the following diagram:

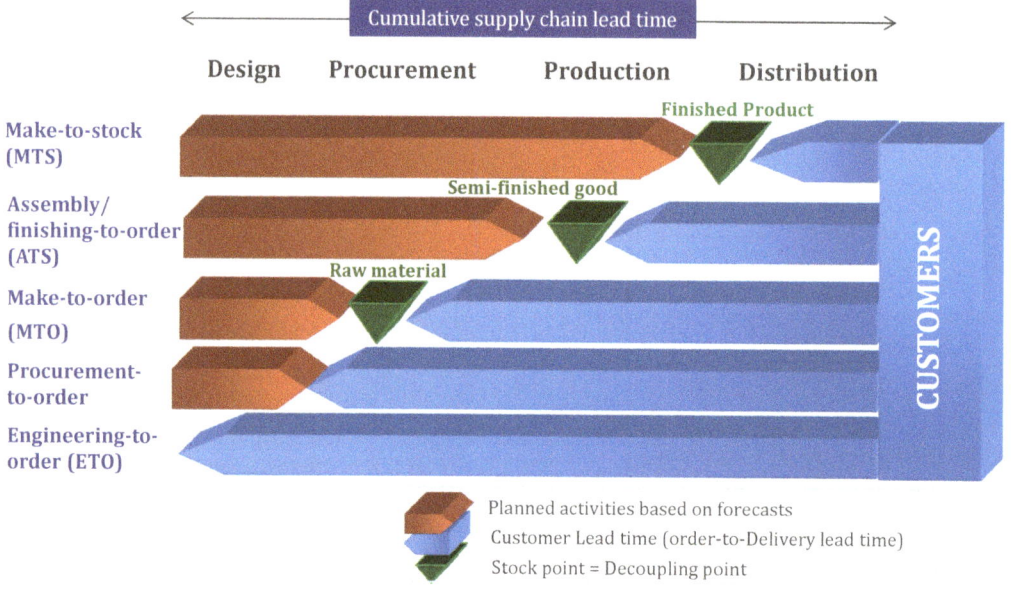

Diag.6: The multiple supply chain strategies

SC planning strategies are the consequence of matching the order-to-delivery lead-time requested by the customers versus the end-to-end supply chain lead-time. The main strategies are the following:

- MTS (Make-to-Stock): if the customer lead-time is much shorter than the E2E SC lead-time, there is no choice: design, procurement and production will have to be anticipated. Based on demand forecast, the finished goods will be produced by anticipation and stored. We hope the pre-built inventories will be meeting the customers' demand. This strategy enables smooth production but requires cash and can generate an obsolence risk.
- ATO (Assembly-to-Order): if the customer lead-time is longer than the previous one, the final production steps such as painting, assembling, finishing and packing do not have to be anticipated and can be made according to the order from the customers.
- MTO (Make-to-Order): in this situation, the longer lead-time requested by the customer enables to produce to order. Nevertheless, long lead-times of some supplied components require holding inventories of raw materials and components. Their consumption has to be forecasted.

- ETO (Engineer-to-Order): for very special orders with a high level of customisation, the full supply chain from design to the delivery has to be done to order.

The consequence has been the development of the **late differentiation model** (or postponed), which is a hybrid model combining MTS upstream and MTO downstream, enabling the benefits of both. We can also call it mass-customisation as MTS generates low-value semi-finished goods with less inventory impact whereas MTO meets a potential requested customisation. The interface separating the two supply chain strategies is called the **decoupling point** as displayed in the following diagram:

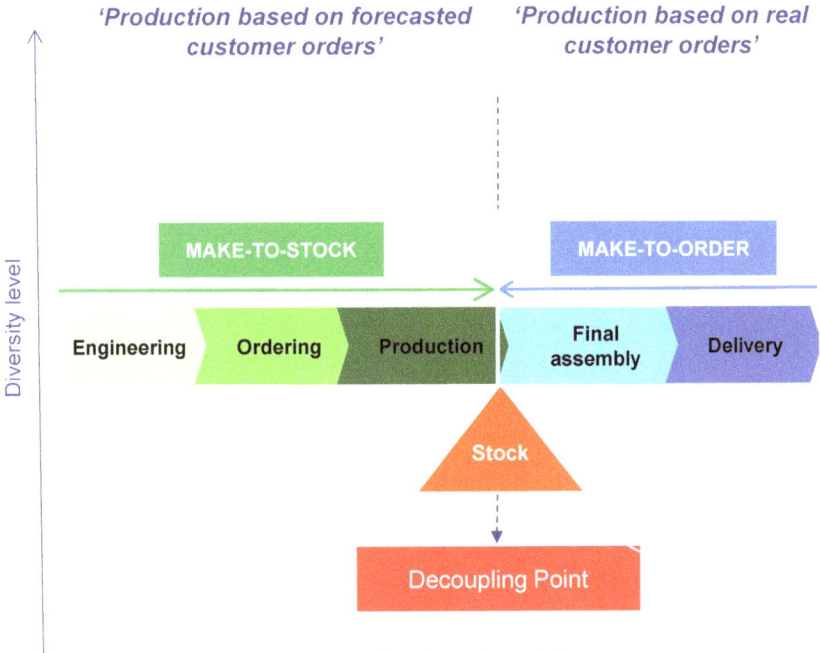

Diag.7: The decoupling point

The level of diversity for the incoming raw materials and components is high and the first part as MTS has the purpose to produce a stock of semi-finished undifferentiated modules at the decoupling point level. Generally, the level of that stock is healthy and risk of obsolescence is low thanks to the low level of diversity of those modules.

As soon as a customer is confirmed, the last steps of production are launched and, due to the potential customisation, the level of diversity can increase a lot.

This hybrid MTS/MTO model originally developed in the computer industry has been deployed in all industries.

## Take-away for leaders

The main take-away for business leaders are to:

- Avoid any confusion between the three definitions we have provided. Very often even at the top level of a company, there is confusion between supply chain management and logistics, what means the perspective given by them is mostly an operational one.

- Model your supply chain in volume, lead-time and finance based on the location of the suppliers, facilities and customers networks in order to test what-if scenarios.

- Adopt a strategic approach to challenge your current supply chain pattern and transform them to increase agility and resilience.

- Test the robustness of your supply chain model and identify its weakest points.

- Apply the methodology of value stream mapping to your supply chain and implement actions to simplify it and to make it more robust.

## Conclusion

The following diagram provides an illustration of the four definitions we have provided:

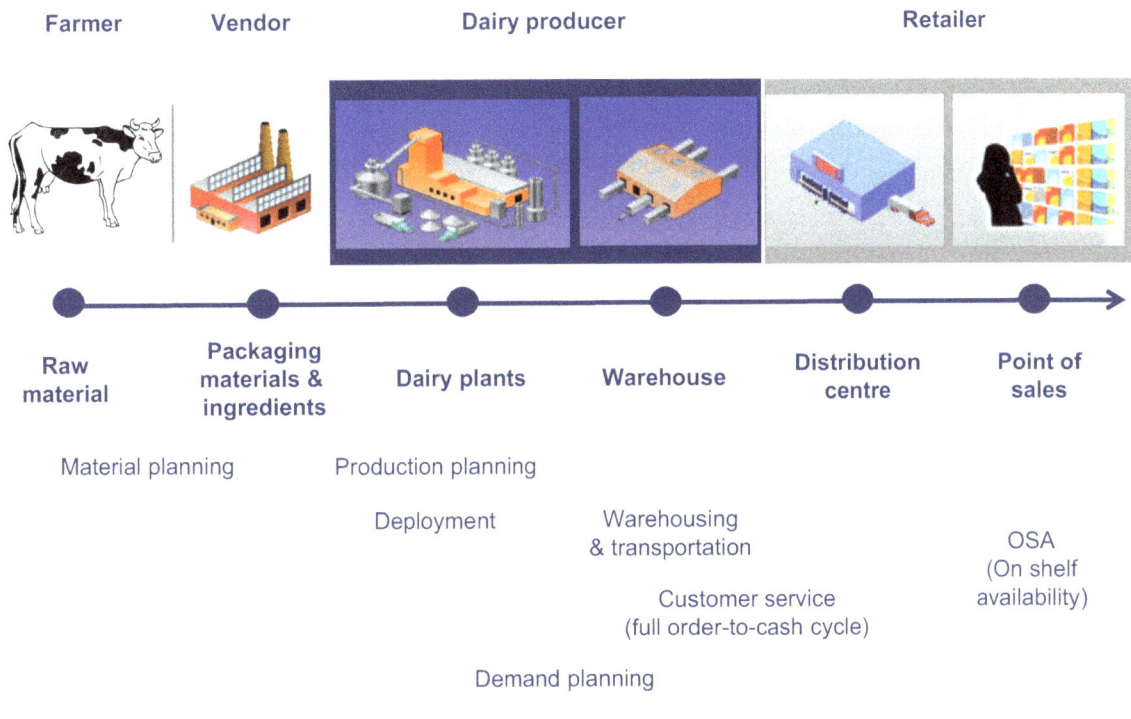

Diag.8: The dairy supply chain

Five main players characterise this dairy product value chain:

- The cows, which provide the raw milk.
- The producers of the complementary and packaging materials such as fruits, ingredients including the flavours, the pots and the covers.
- The producer of the dairy products. Their own value chain covers product innovation, marketing, production and logistics.
- The retailers' value chain includes their logistics facilities and their points of sales (POS).
- Finally, the shoppers visiting the POS or placing orders online.

Part A Use SCM to generate business value

The application of the former three definitions shows:

- A fragmented supply chain, each main player being focused on their own main value-added activity and a local–local supply chain model due to the low value of the products and the pressure on the product shelf life.
- Logistics is everywhere within each player (inside the plants and the logistics facilities) and between each of them.
- OSA (On Shelf Availability) assesses the supply chain management performance, and the demand plan process is based on the sell-out to the final consumers and not on the sell-in.

> ### Key questions to address
>
> 1. Have you identified and assessed the main vulnerabilities and the risks of your supply chain model? Then, have you evaluated its resilience?
> 2. Have you estimated the end-to-end SC lead-time?
> 3. Have you calculated the number of players involved in your end-to-end SC model and the potential complexity?
> 4. How many supply chain patterns do you manage?
> 5. Have you estimated the volatility of both supply and demand sides of your SC model and identified the solutions to face it?
> 6. Have you measured the total amount of inventories along the full end-to-end SC and especially the inventories in your internal SC?
> 7. Have you tested the agility of your supply chain management?
> 8. Have you clear supply chain planning strategies according to segmentation variables?
> 9. Have you used the decoupling point to design your supply chains?
> 10. How do you measure the level of service: at the exit of your warehouse (shipped), at the entrance of your customer warehouse (delivered) or at the point of sales of your customer (OSA)?

# Chapter 1
# The five-parameter value equation of supply chain

## Key ideas

SCM can contribute to the creation of five types of value:

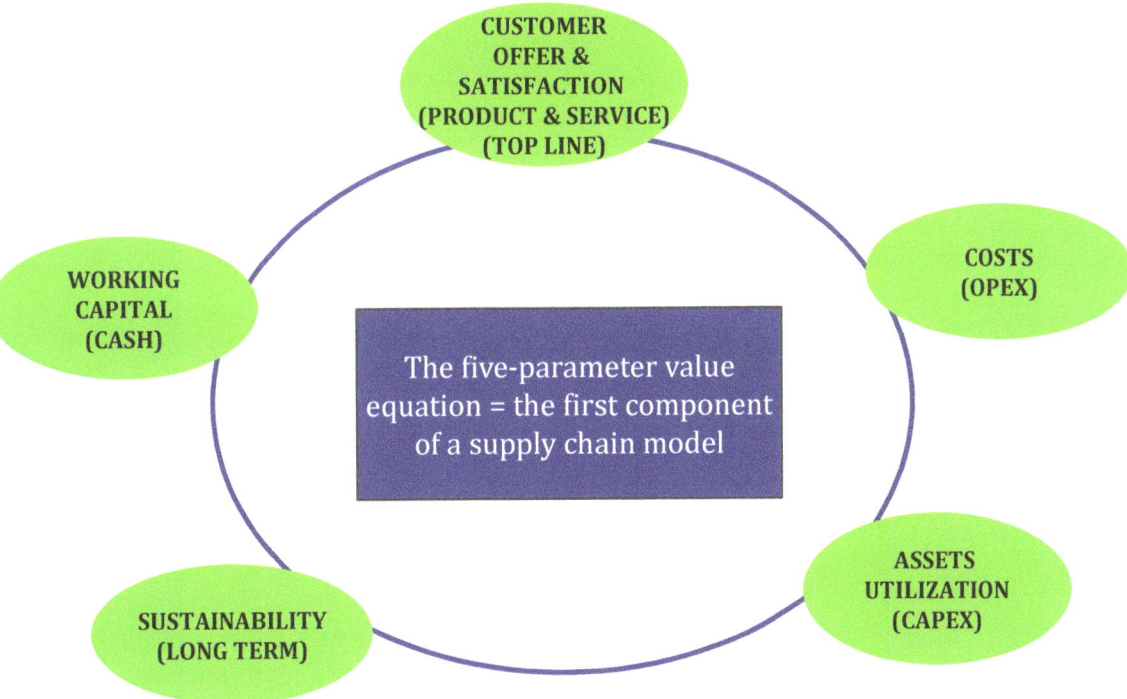

Diag.1: The five-parameter value equation of supply chain

## 1. Customer offer and satisfaction

SCM is the activity in charge of executing the promise to customers. The excellence of service is equal to customer perception minus customer expectation. Prior to their delivery, the offers have to be designed. To do so, this is necessary to hear a triple VOC meaning:

- The Voice of the Customers to avoid providing an over service, which will generate a higher cost-to-serve.
- The Voice of the Competitors to run a competitive benchmark from both direct and indirect competitors.
- The Voice of the CEO to consider the strategic market positioning, especially in terms of priorities related to innovation, cost and customer intimacy.

The definition of the offers formalised within service charters generally at the country level and service level agreements for the key accounts will be done through a collaborative process involving marketing, product development and supply chain stakeholders. The validation of them has to be under the leader's accountability as explained in Chapter 2.

The major KPIs related to this first value parameter are:

- Net Promoter Score (NPS) as the main KPI to measure the perceived value by the customers and its customer experience components.
- On Time in Full (OTIF) measured at the order level.
- Time-to-Market for the introduction of the new products.
- The number of products you offer to the market.
- Quality non-conformity and its connection to the claims from dissatisfied customers.

## 2. Cost

The level of the recurrent costs within the end-to-end supply chain depends on multiple factors, and their impact on the P&L under the leader's control can be highly significant.
    The end-to-end supply chain cost has to be analysed into its components of cost-to-source, cost-to-produce and cost-to-serve. SCM is the natural function to provide such financial analysis as covered in Chapter 3.

## 3. Working capital

SCM impacts the three components of the working capital:

- The inventories composed of the raw materials, the semi-finished goods and the produced or traded finished goods. Management of the inventories has a level of complexity, which has not to be underestimated, and the input from the leaders is key as we will see in Chapter 4.
- The receivables belong to the order-to-cash process and some companies have made supply chain accountable for speeding up this cycle.
- The payables to the suppliers rely on the procurement strategy according to the profiles of those suppliers, which have to be assessed with the same KPIs used for measuring the customers' satisfaction.

SCM value is to optimise the cash level frozen within those three components and the rotation of those cycle assets. For the inventories, this financial perspective is completed by a supply chain objective linking the level of inventories with the level of service delivered to the customers to meet the service promise.

## 4. Assets utilisation

The industrial (plants) and the logistics (distribution centres, depots, warehouses, platforms, transportation means) assets consume a lot of CAPEX. In the past, independent stakeholders managed those assets: sales teams were talking directly to the plant managers to negotiate volume and price and to logistics managers to decide where to store the finished goods. Due to the interconnection of the production and logistics facilities within global networks, a central supply chain team plays the role of interfacing the demand side and the supply side of much more fragmented and global supply chains.

The value provided by SCM is to ensure the best utilisation of those assets measured by the OEE (Overall Equipment Efficiency) and the lowest inventory and transportation costs by allocating the customers' demand and planning inventories and production workload. The benefits of such approach are detailed in Chapter 5 and the way of implementing cross-functional collaborative processes in Chapter 13.

In terms of performance tracking, the CAPEX level and the ROI (Return On Investments) are the most important.

## 5. Sustainability

SCM potentially contributes to the three components of sustainability:

- People: in Chapters 7 and 13, we will explain how SCM, as the most cross-functional process in any company, supports the development of One Team in order to ensure the convergence of the executive committee members. This is a key value to build up a united team able to work on natural contradictory conflicts.
- Planet: SCM generates one of the biggest impacts in terms of carbon footprints, especially with the development of global end-to-end supply chains including the growth of e-commerce.
- Profit: in a VUCA (volatile, uncertain, complex, ambiguous) environment, SCM supports a long-term profit by mitigating the multiple risks global supply chains face.

For each of those five value parameters, SCM has the following roles:

- Take part in the definition of the target value for each of the five value parameters.
- Design the most appropriate solutions to achieve those objectives.
- Be accountable for generating the expected value.
- Report on the achieved performance.

# The five parameter value equation of supply chain

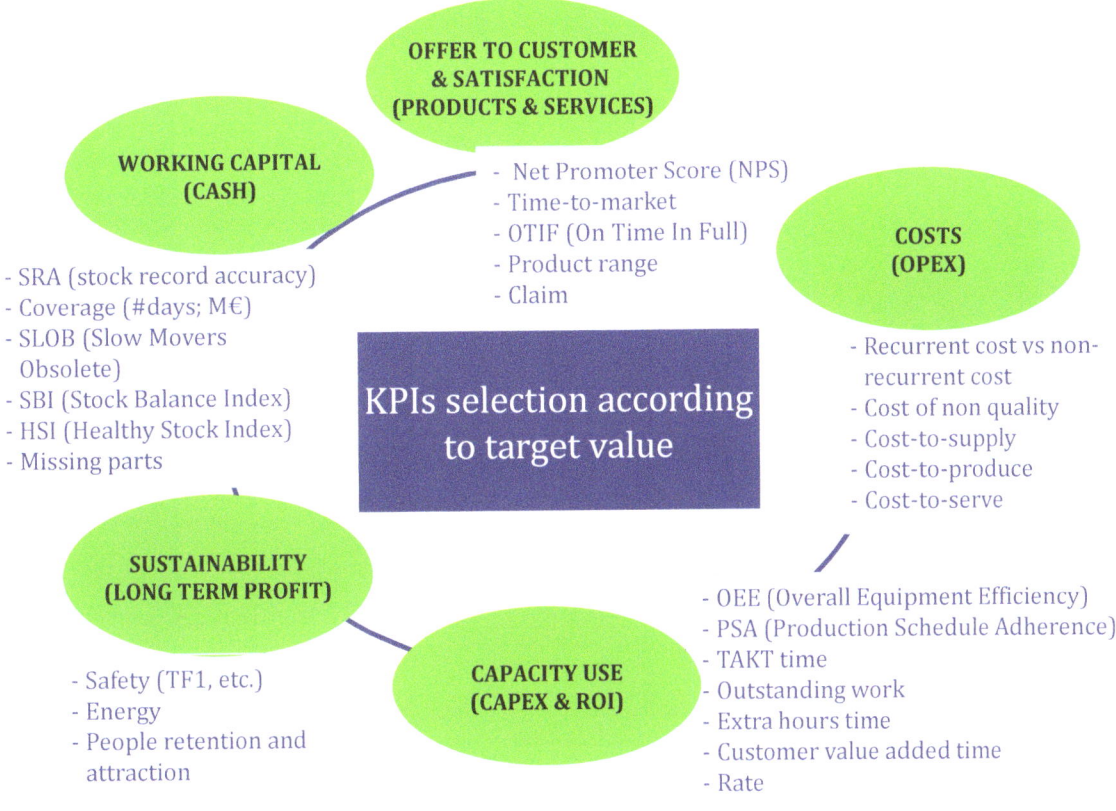

Diag.2: The main KPIs of the value creation by SCM

# Testimony from Essilor International

Paul du SAILLANT, Chief Executive Officer, Essilor International

Eric JAVELLAUD, Senior VP Global Supply Chain & Prescription Operations Strategy, Sourcing and Procurement, Essilor International

*What are the main business challenges of Essilor?*

Essilor designs, manufactures and markets a wide range of lenses to improve and protect eyesight. In fact, everything we do is driven by our mission of improving lives by improving sight.

To serve this mission, across all our activities, Essilor's strategy rests on four main pillars:

- innovating in products, services and technology, thereby enabling the introduction of products every year that deliver improved performance and benefits to new wearers, to address unresolved vision problems.
- developing solutions tailored to every segment and every geography in order to meet the diverse needs of eyecare professionals and consumers. It has been made possible as the company has a global network model made up of prescription labs, logistics hubs, and R&D centres.
- acquiring new companies and forming partnerships with industry stakeholders, to deepen our local presence or enhance our asset portfolio.
- stimulating demand by deploying vision awareness programs, screening campaigns and initiatives to make visual correction more widely accessible.

These four pillars are supported by sustainable manufacturing and operational efficiency along with a deep commitment to corporate social responsibility.

*How does supply chain management provide value and performance to the business?*

Essilor has an open business model wherein products and services are made available in a growing number of geographies and locations.

The first business value that Essilor's supply chain provides is the best proximity service to its customers. Therefore, Essilor has developed an extended footprint of facilities consisting of:

- A network of 455 prescription laboratories and edging-mounting centres spread across the world, including eight large server laboratories, which produce lenses mainly for the Asian, European and North American markets.
- Five integrated lenses and frames platforms. These platforms were developed as part of integrated service offerings for large accounts, which include the manufacture of lenses, the management of frames on behalf of customers and, in some cases, the edging and mounting of lenses in glasses.
- Fourteen distribution centres.

This value includes the product offer to customers, while digitalisation drives Essilor's global supply chain dedicated to producing and delivering over 550 million lenses a year with a high degree of personalisation for individual wearers.

Essilor's supply chain covers all the global flows of the Group's products/lenses, from production sites to points of sale for eye care practitioner, including stock units central and prescription laboratories. Then, the second value is to optimise the cost-to-serve, while managing the new products introduction and guaranteeing service continuity plans.

Essilor also continues to reduce cash utilisation by:

- Reducing inventory level year after year. It has continued to make progress in terms of inventory days and inventory value despite the increase in output.
- Better managing the supply chain assets thanks to efficiency programs such as lean manufacturing, and consolidation.

**What are the main consequences from the supply chain perspective of the merger with Luxottica?**

With the ultimate objective of building a unified company, EssilorLuxottica has launched more than 20 priority work streams and 160 business initiatives that are being implemented globally to drive the integration and deliver synergies.

One of the first steps is the creation of one single supply chain and prescription laboratories network.

This creation needs to:

- Regroup in one single network all the Essilor Labs and Luxottica labs.
- Standardise all industrial processes to allow the same capabilities.
- Unify management processes such as S&OP, flow routings and the introduction of new products.
- Better manage and combine frames and lenses with the objective to better serve our customers and develop the complete pair offers (frame and lenses).

*Eric, as the senior VP of supply chain director of Essilor you are in charge as well of Rx operations, and purchasing, could you explain the benefits of such an organisation?*

The advantage of such an organisation is to have all the levers to create and improve the operating models that bring value to customers. We can cite for example the implementation of the online model and the omnichannel, or the management of integrated supply chain for a key account.

### How does Essilor's supply chain contribute to the sustainable development?

Essilor's approach to sustainable development is based on the consideration of the environmental, social and societal impacts of our business activities on our various stakeholders all along the value chain, in line with its mission to improve lives by improving sight.

In line with these commitments, in 2018, Essilor's production plants pursued efforts to reduce their water and energy consumption in an effort to meet the company's objectives of achieving by 2020 a 20% reduction in water use per lens produced and a 15% cut in energy intensity per lens produced relative to the 2015 levels.

The supply chain monitors $CO_2$ emissions from upstream and downstream transport and leads the reduction of emissions through the optimisation of transport flows and the search for an alternative to airplanes (e.g. Air to Sea).

The supply chain also has the willingness to develop a waste reduction program through packaging optimisation, and to set new targets by 2025.

## Take-away for leaders

SCM impacts directly the generation of five values to the business: customer satisfaction, OPEX, cash, CAPEX and sustainability. We call it the five-parameter value equation of SCM.

For each of them, the definition of the value target is fundamentally under the decision of the top management. Even if supply chain managers will be accountable for delivering those values, leaders have to provide their input in terms of the strategy that SCM will serve.

The strategic market positioning (innovation, cost, customer intimacy) is a key driver for defining the right selection of the values out of the five-parameter value equation. This selection and the value objectives formalise the value roadmap of your business model and we call it the value proposition of your supply chain model, which will be operationalised in Chapter 10.

SCM has the most cross-player activity within the company, interfacing the multiple functions of an executive committee and within the value network involving the multiple suppliers, contractors, third party logistics, distributors and customers.

SCM plays the role of facilitating the interface management of those players in order to get a convergence between them at both value objective definition and operational execution.

Part A  Use SCM to generate business value

## Key questions to address

1. Do you consider SCM as a leverage of your business model? If yes, in which perspectives?
2. Do you consider SCM as a pure support activity or as a business activity?
3. Which business value out of the five-parameter value equation do you expect from SCM?
4. What are your business priorities in terms of value creation?
5. Have you formalised a supply chain value roadmap?
6. Do you face regular conflicts at your executive committee?
7. Do you involve SCM in your value roadmap definition?
8. Do you involve key suppliers and key customers to formalise your value roadmap?
9. Have you defined formal accountabilities to your SCM team?

# Chapter 2
# Boost your top line by developing customer satisfaction

## Key ideas

Three complementary axes support the contribution of SCM to the top line:

## 1. Developing offers to customers

The first value of the leadership model of Amazon Web Services (AWS) is 'customer obsession', highlighting the fact most new ideas of offers to customers come from the customers themselves.

The offers have to be designed according to the VOC[3] involving collaborative marketing, sales and supply chain managers as explained in Chapter 1. An offer is made of products, services and channels lists.

In terms of products, the major dimension supply chain managers pay attention to is the number of SKUs (items), which are offered. This is a strategic marketing decision, which impacts the market positioning of the supplier, complementary to the price decision. As we will see in Chapter 10, the higher number of items you offer, the more complex the supply chain management will be.

The top five services you can offer in B2B and B2C businesses are:

- The **order-to-delivery lead-time.** Customers are highly sensitive to the lead-time, which is required to get their ordered products. Here this is question of both the speed and the respect of it according to the promise a supplier has made. This first service component is assessed by the OTD (On Time Delivery).
- The respect of the **quantity and the quality** ($Q^2$) of the delivered products. This second service component is assessed by the fill rate. This quantity is linked to the possible rebates related to the sold volume.

- The **frequency of deliveries.** This service attribute impacts both the logistics cost and the product stock level:
    * The more frequently you deliver, the lower quantity you deliver, the more expensive the delivery cost will be. This is the bad news.
    * But the more frequently you deliver, the lower the stock level will be at the customer site. This, then, is a key element, which depends for instance on the storage capacity of the customer, their sensitivity to cash and the transportation cost.
- The **cut off time,** which is the latest time a customer can place an order on a daily basis. If you don't respect this cut off time, you will be losing as a customer one day of delivery lead-time.
- The **returns.** This is a growing component attribute with the booming online business. The question as a supplier is to know if you accept or not a free return of goods from your customers, keeping in mind that from a legal point of view, at least in the EU, this is right to the customer to return goods ordered by online channels.

Of course, the list of the potential services you can offer to a customer is a long one and the selection of them should follow the three main steps in the customer journey:

- Pre-order: support documentation and information access, samples, benchmarking for product selection, quotation process, technical and marketing support.
- Order: manual vs automated order process, stock visibility, minimum order quantity (mOQ), planning of delivery time, advanced shipment notification (ASN), shipment documentation, order tracking.
- After-sales service: claims tracking, return conditions, single point of contact, waste and after-use recycling.

Those offers have to be formalised in service charters and in service level agreements for key accounts including potential penalties if the service is not fulfilled.

## 2. Meeting customer expectations and getting customer loyalty

As we introduced in Chapter 1, SCM is the activity in charge of executing the promise to the customers, and then generating a unique customer experience. Meeting customer expectations has to go through metrics, which enable objective measurement of the performance of the delivered experience to those customers.

The main KPI related to the top line SCM is accountable for is OTIF: On Time In Full. We will see in Chapter 11 the different ways of calculating it, but this KPI is a hybrid mixing the achieved performance of the top two above listed service components. This is a percentage looking at the order level, how good you were at delivering OTIF on that order. This way of assessing customer experience is a very rational one but this is insufficient and has to be completed by the fundamental notion of perception.

As shown in diagram 1, the first issue is the gap of the requested OTIF by the customer and what after-negotiation has been promised to them. Very few ERP systems follow the first request of the customers and just keep a trace on a confirmed order with the promised OTD. Therefore, the OTIF assessment is a 'fake' one. But worse than that, even if there is no gap between requested, promised and achieved OTIF, at the end of the day some customers don't consider you as their preferred supplier. Why? Just because of the wrong perception along the customer journey. This is why another KPI, which was so far used by marketing, has to be now analysed by SCM: the NPS. It means that the notion of supplier preference is not only based on rational facts but as well on emotional perceptions. An NPS decline is a very strong signal for the top line and often a lack of SCM awareness by business leaders.

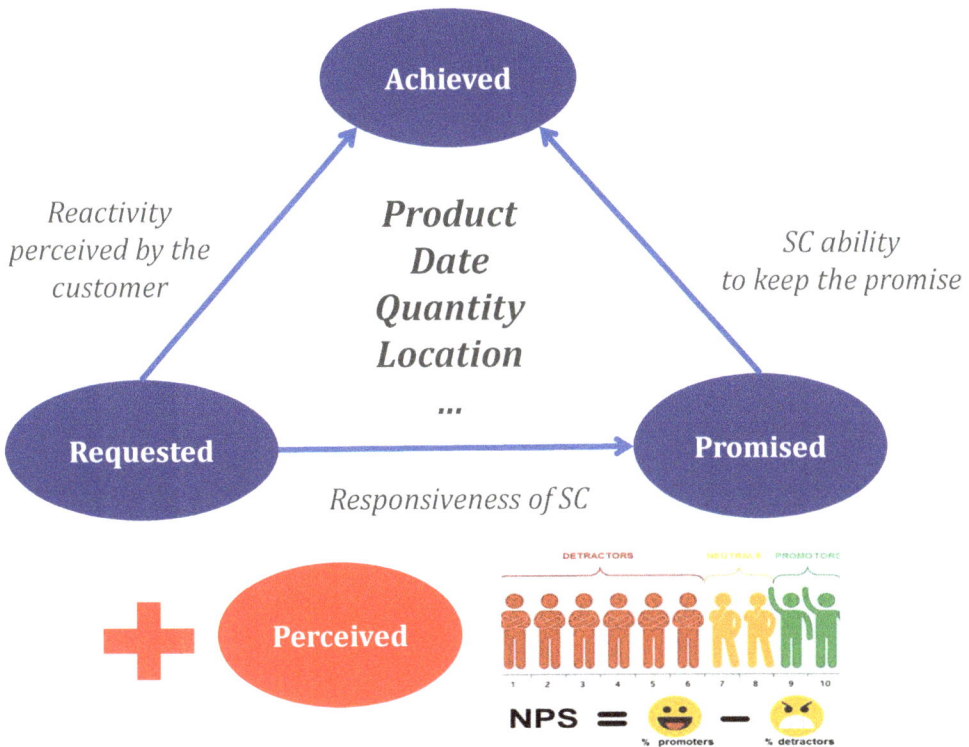

Diag.1: The notion of perceived value by customers

Part A  Use SCM to generate business value

The access cost for getting new customers, the cost of customer attrition and the value of loyal customers are central to consider.

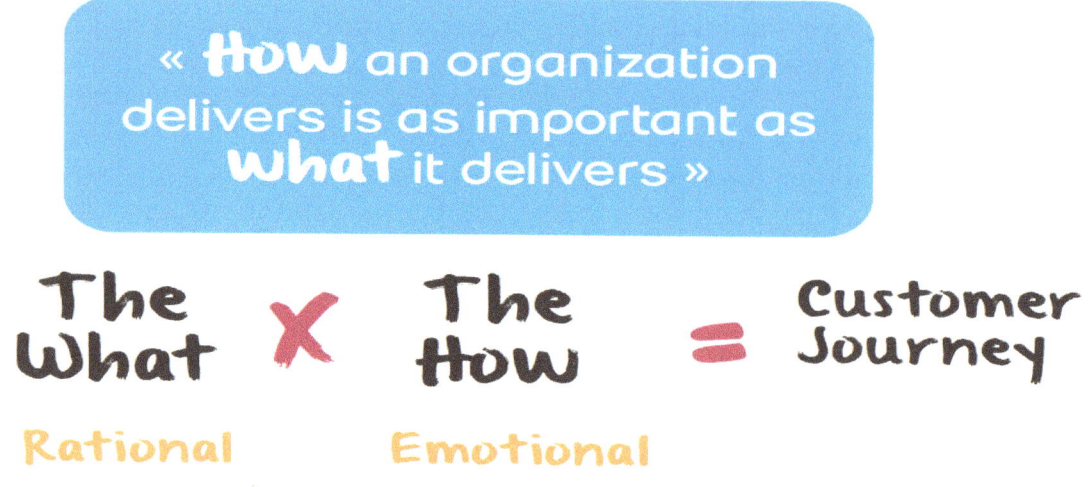

Diag.2: Supply chain management has to generate emotion

The role played by the customer service department is critical in that value delivery.

## 3. Segmenting the offers

Increasing the value delivered to customers relies as well on segmenting it according, for instance, to the profiles of customers. Generally, marketing and sales strategies segment them in three ABC categories such as: strategic customers, invest to grow customers and opportunistic customers. Consistently, potential services can be segmented into three categories:

– Basic services: standard lead-time, automated order process by EDI, VMI (Vendor Managed Inventory), back-order management, minimum order quantity, order status tracking.
– Advanced or premium services: consignment and safety stock, delivery to each single point of sales (i.e. direct to customer delivery), returns management, tailored packaging, rush delivery based on express transportation.
– Integrated services: customer assortment management, collaborative forecast.

Keep in mind that a given service can be considered basic for one customer but advanced for another, and that segmentation depends on your competitive positioning and on your industry itself.

The consequences of those segmented offers on the supply chain model will be explained in the Chapter 12.

# Testimony from 3M

Pierre MORAND, Supply Reporting Lead for EMEA, 3M

Laurence RATCLIFFE, Service Lead Key Accounts for EMEA Consumer Business, 3M

*Can you introduce the business of 3M?*

3M (Minnesota Mining Manufacturing) is a diversified conglomerate headquartered in St Paul MN in the USA and part of the Dow Jones. 3M has 90,000 employees operating in 70 countries with manufacturing facilities in 35 of them.

3M is well known for consumer brands such as Post It® notes or Scotch® tape, but the company is acting in many diversified markets articulated around four businesses: safety and industrial, transportation and electronics, healthcare and consumer. We invest 6% of the turnover in R&D and the portfolio includes 117,000 patents. Individual technologies are spread across businesses to offer around 55,000 products. As a summary 3M is 'Sciences applied to Life™'.

3M values cover Inclusion, diversity, sustainability and 3M has been recognised as part of the World's Most Ethical Companies in 2019. The company is engaged in a sustainability program since 1975 and was present at the Cop25 in Madrid in 2019.

*What are the main business challenges?*

After the 2008 crisis the company has engaged some important changes along with business and product portfolio rationalisation. On top of this the company has engaged a program to deploy a common ERP all across EMEA. The company has started to see the benefits of such an investment; this includes centralised master data creation and governance, common language and common standard work on each site. This has also provided the ability to start collecting harmonised data in a single warehouse opening doors to new value creation.

*What are the main actions you have implemented to generate such expected value?*

With the deployment of the new ERP, reporting started back from a blank page. A new data intelligence department has been created to support the value creation of exploiting these data. The main challenge was not to reproduce what was existing in Legacy before but to develop solutions based on the new processes. A lot of time has been spent to train users on understanding the changes. Development scope has included dashboard creation to support KPIs for management but also the ability to drill down to material ID level to track the root causes of deviation to target.

A strong and structured hoppering process for prioritisation and validation with all teams supports reporting solution delivery. When approve,d the development is done using 'agile methodology' principle. All the dashboards and reports centrally 'certified' can be found on a single 'reporting portal' with security accesses based on the roles defined in the ERP.

*Could you give some examples of KPIs and digitalisation?*

A lot of effort has been put to develop KPIs around service to customers including back-order rates, product availability and OTIF'. Attached to that, some logic has been defined to drill down on the root causes of missed OTIF to properly address the issues. Work is currently done to move from measuring these metrics when we ship to measuring when we deliver in order to get closer to the way our customers are measuring our performance. The key challenge is to feed back in our system the delivery date coming from the POD (proof of delivery) message sent back by our carriers.

Another example is the integration of the 'point of sales' information coming from our distributors so that we can integrate these in our data warehouse. Comprehensive dashboards have been built out of these so that our sales rep could share performance in a nice way when visiting the distributors, since these are easily available on mobile equipment.

*Do you consider data as a strategic driver in terms of value creation?*

To bring value to users and make new solution successful, it has been key to include in the report design analytical functionalities and not pure descriptive trending charts. It helps to go straight to the point. After that, with the expertise gained on each stream the next step has been to work on developing a predictive tool. With combined effort between process experts, data analytics and the operational planning team, 3M has developed its own set of dashboards to support the five steps of IBP, an enhanced version of S&OP. This dashboard includes forecasts accuracy KPIs and enables us to switch from value to units. These cross-functional reports are now in the list of the most used in the company.

*What are the benefits of S&OP you have implemented?*

This IBP process is used to analyse discrepancies between financial targets and what is coming out of the ERP planning system, taking into consideration optimised forecasts and netted supply plans. The advantage of having a single ERP including manufacturing MRP system is that it is providing the ability to focus on constraint work centres (the bottlenecks) to solve planning issues and rebalance the load. Having the reporting tools in place helps to support the discussions to reach consensus based on facts and data in order to better serve customers.

*What are the characteristics of your customers and your distribution channels?*

As said in the company introduction, 3M is serving very diversified markets from automotive and aerospace industries, to fast moving goods consumer goods including direct deliveries to the pharmacy at your street corner. The company is 'omnichannel' which is representing many challenges to adapt the supply chain to each of these.

*What example of action has been taken to leverage the customer service strategy?*

3M has created new key account service lead positions to support strategic customers. These persons are working hand to hand with the key account sales managers. Their task is to discuss continuous improvement with the customers covering supply chain and service quality. One key element for them is to build intimacy with the customer contacts to create trust and partnership for win/win solutions. The service leads can anticipate the changes and needs from the customers and advocate these internally by aligning 3M resources to serve the customers. With the customer insight they get, the service leads are able to improve forecasts, stock sizing and offer-improved support to the 'phase in/phase out' activities, which are always a challenge. The initiative and team have proven to really bring values. As an example, 3M as received the SQIP Award 'Best Performer 2019' from Airbus.

*What are the main results of the supply chain excellence program?*

In the past there were several ERP used in Europe, making it complicated to aggregate reporting solutions and KPIs, as well as getting end-to-end visibility. Having deployed a single ERP with all data in, one warehouse is now providing the capability to implement a single source of the trough with standard harmonised KPIs and dashboard solutions together with end-to-end visibility. An internal IBP reporting solution has been developed. All this is offering a strong support to new position such as the service leads in the business who can access data easily when working on improvement plans with customers.

After a transition period the service is now back to target. Backorders have been decreased by 30% with inventories being well controlled. Other regions in the world that have not yet made this move to a single ERP are very much interested in the European experience!

## Take-away for leaders

The impact of SCM on the top line is multiple:

– Avoid losing customers due to a lack of promised service delivery.

– Avoid missing sales due to shortage of products.

– Keep customers loyal and enable them to identify you as their preferred supplier.

– Develop new ways including new distribution channels to reach customers.

– Offer advanced services providing value to customers and enabling extra revenue.

– Propose spot offers to stimulate sales.

## Key questions to address

1. Have you implemented a systematic customer service survey enabling you to measure OTIF and NPS?
2. Have you formalised your offer on service charter at the appropriate cluster and service level agreement for your key accounts?
3. Have you analysed the causes of the NPS level and its links to SCM?
4. Have you mapped the customer journey and identified specific services for each step?
5. Have you developed advanced services to generate extra revenues?
6. What is the level of collaboration between the marketing and supply chain managers?
7. Do you have a segmented offer of services?
8. Do you price extra services?

# Chapter 3
# Minimise the cost-to-serve

## Key ideas

### 1. The components of the end-to-end supply chain cost (E2E SC cost)

The end-to-end supply chain cost covers three main domains as diagram 1 shows:

**Total End-to-End Supply Chain Cost**

| Cost-to-supply | | Cost-to-produce | Cost-to-serve | | |
|---|---|---|---|---|---|
| Supply (€/kg or €/pal) | Upstream storage (€/kg or pal) | Production (€/kg or pal) | Downstream storage (€/kg or pal) | Distribution (€/kg or pal or order) | Delivery (€/kg or pal or order) |
| Sourcing | Receiving goods | Labour | Picking | Outbound transportation | Last mile |
| Inbound transportation | Physical and financial storage | Maintenance and repair | Packing | Cross-docking | Samples and outlet display |
| Customs and duties | Obsolete and scrap | Energy | Obsolete and scrap | Customs and duties | On-shelf handling |

 Returns of goods and waste recycling costs
Demand and production planning, inventory management, order management and customer service: teams and information systems

Diag.1: The components of the cost-to-serve

- The **cost-to-supply**, which is related to the sourcing of raw materials, components and trade goods from external suppliers. Its proportion depends on your make or buy policy and the product value structure, but it can be from 20% to 60% of the full finished good value and even more in case of a fragmented value chain.

It includes the upfront purchasing cost, which may or may not include the upstream logistics costs according to the incoterms of the sourcing contract negotiated with the supplier. This upstream logistics cost covers packing, handling, transportation and delivery. Beyond that, customs and duties in case of international sourcing have to be considered as well as the cost generated by the obsolescence of slow movers goods and the potential scraps of them. Clearly a good/low sourcing cost from Best Cost Countries can be counterbalanced by the logistics costs. Supply chain managers have to be involved in the sourcing process in a collaborative mode with the buyers to evaluate the full cost-to-supply in order not only to build a feasible and robust upstream logistics solution but also to validate the economic value of that sourcing solution.

The cost-to-supply has to be analysed as well according to the criticality of the sourced part (single source, expensive part, consequence of a shortage, supply lead-time, etc.) and the expected service, which has to be specified in the tenders.

- The **cost-to-produce** is related to the value in-house you add to the product. This cost breakdown depends on the level of labour (cost, skills) vs machinery (automation) and how capital intensive your production model is. Therefore, the labour cost depends on the location of the production facilities, keeping in mind the labour rate between Mexico and USA is 1 to 10 and in Europe between Romania and Germany 1 to 6 (2019 data). The sourcing of energy can also be a decision criterion of locating a plant in terms of both availability and cost.
- The **cost-to-serve** covers the downstream part of the supply chain from the production facilities to the customers. The biggest cost is the last mile delivery, which explodes with the online channel and includes packaging and transportation. But the picking cost can represent a big part too, and drove the evolution of the picking from man-to-good model to good-to-man model as explained in the introduction of Part A. In case of global/local-to-global supply chain patterns, customs and duties have to be added.

As for the cost-to-supply, obsolescence and scraps weigh on the cost-to-serve. Complementary to the finished goods, the supply of samples and POS materials for merchandising products can add a lot of cost-to-serve due to the number of items and the fact that generally this cost is not charged to the customers.

In case of late differentiation, some value-added post-manufacturing operations such as customisation, kitting and packaging can be done in the downstream logistics facilities.

The costs we listed above are operational costs. In order to get the full end-to-end cost, people in charge of demand planning, production planning, logistics planning, stock management, reporting, order management and customer service management have to be included as well as the information systems, which support those operations at both decision (tactical) and operational levels.

In addition to those costs, the after-sales supply chain generates additional costs in order to cover the cost of the packaging returns (pallets, cartons), the returned unsold goods and the waste management including the dismantling process and the generation of secondary materials.

Those end-to-end supply chain costs have to be measured as a percentage of the product value. For evaluating the product value, we recommend using a unit value such as:

- €/kg or €/ton. For instance, the sales value of a cell phone can be 500 €/kg i.e. 500 k€/ton whereas mineral water is 1.5 k€/ton, and high-value raw flat glass around 0.725 k€/ton and basic raw glass 0.45 k€/ton.
- €/unit.
- €/pallet for FMCG products such as dry food or €/roll.
- €/$m^3$ for light products such as insulation, toilet paper, etc.
- €/$m^2$ for products with large surface such as glass, plaster board, etc.
- €/order line.

The product value expressed at a unit level per a technical item such as the weight, the piece, the pallet (which is the logistics unit for many businesses), $m^3$ or $m^2$ is a fundamental approach and leads to the supply chain model choice as explained in the introduction of Part A. This is also relevant to the price rate used by the carriers and the 3PL (third party logistics), who charge their services according to the volume.

Rare are the companies that have developed an accurate way to evaluate their end-to-end supply chain costs, especially because of the silo organisation, the reporting structure in terms of cost versus profit centres and often the lack of IT integration along the supply chain. In most cases, this is only a fragmented evaluation, which is taken out and focused on the logistics costs without sourcing and production. Then, if we focus on the logistics costs, transportation is definitely the biggest part (close to 50% of the full logistics cost), the warehousing (storage and picking close to 20%), the holding inventory cost (another 20%) and the rest for administration. A full chain margin approach developed by financial managers is a good way.

## 2. The drivers of the end-to-end supply chain cost

Our experience with our customers shows that the notion of cost driver is not well known. When I ask the question, 'What are the drivers of your end-to-end supply chain costs?' I generally received an answer like 'The biggest part of the cost is transportation.' There is a potential confusion about the cost proportion and the cost drivers, which is a problem, as cost control should work essentially on the drivers.

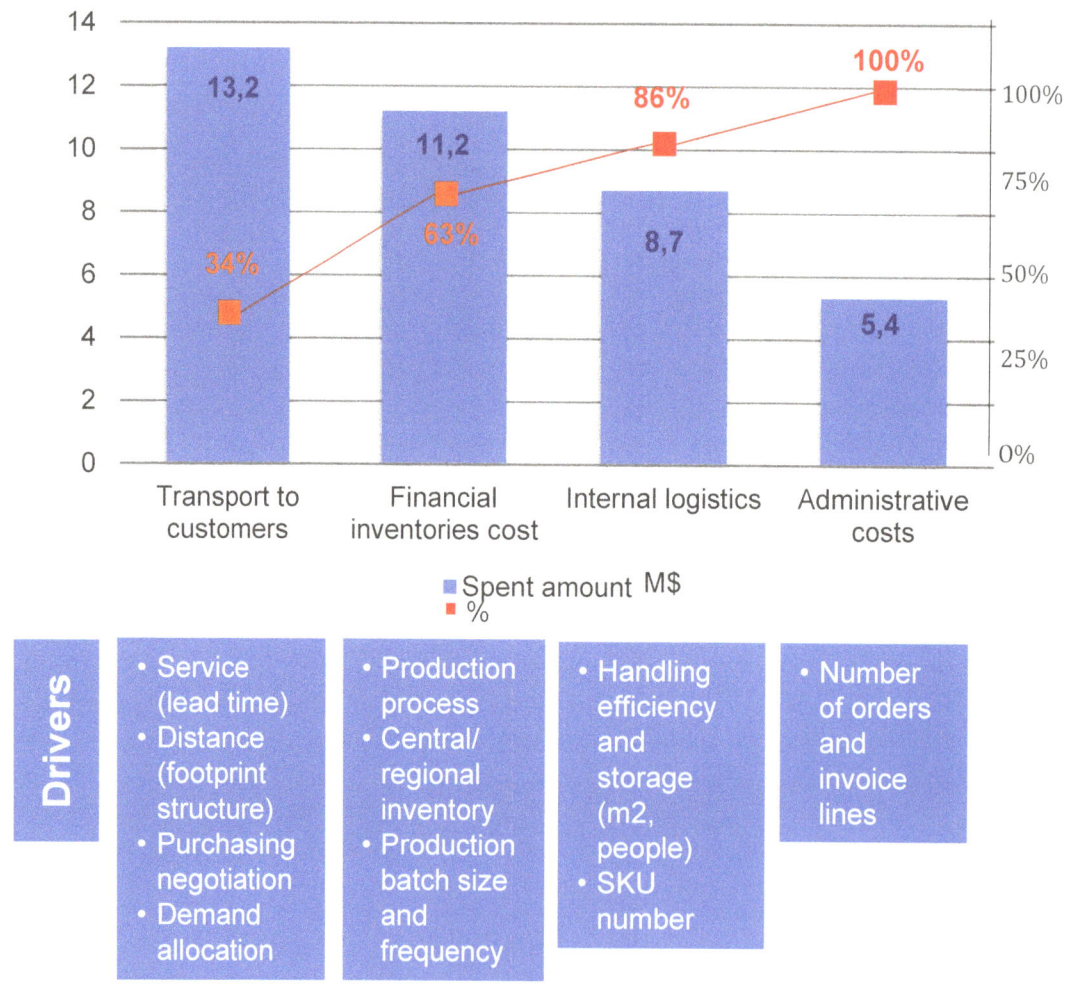

Diag.2: The drivers of the cost-to-serve

The second diagram shows an example in a commodity industry with a list of the main drivers:

- The most important driver is the **offer** you have decided to market to your customers and especially the number of SKUs and the lead-time. The higher number of SKUs and the faster the delivery lead-time is (like rush order), the more expensive the E2E SC cost is.
- The **distance**, which depends on the SC model you have designed, is a major driver. The location of the suppliers, the plants, the distribution centres and the point of sales have a direct impact on the E2E SC cost. This distance depends as well on the allocation of the demand to a given plant if several plants have the same capability to produce such demand.
- The **volume** along the supply chain. The economic equation of SCM highly depends on the frequency (as seen in Chapter 2) of produced or shipped products (batch size in both cases). This volume depends on minimum order quantities, which have been negotiated with the suppliers for the cost-to-supply, the plant managers for the cost-to-produce and the customers for the cost-to-serve.
- The type of the production and the logistics solutions including the **technology** (good-to-man) and the level of **automation**, but as we will see in Chapter 5, this driver has an impact as well on CAPEX.
- The **order profile** in terms of the number of order lines and the ordered volume per line is another driver impacting a lot the picking cost.

# Testimony from Trinseo

Tim STEDMAN, Senior VP Strategy Director, Trinseo

Pierre CHORAND, Global Supply Chain Director, Trinseo

*What are the main business challenges of your business?*

Trinseo is a global materials solutions provider and a manufacturer of plastics, latex binders, and synthetic rubber. Overall, competition is increasing, affecting primarily commodity markets. For example, we are seeing some petrochemical conglomerates moving down the value chain as vertical integration gives them a competitive advantage on the feedstock prices. Moreover, key Asian players are becoming larger both within the region and extending their presence globally, especially into Europe. This is intensifying the competitive environment with overcapacity and downward pressure on prices. This is all further exacerbated when overall demand is weak.

Another characteristic of our business is the volatility of raw material prices and the cyclical nature of some segments, like polycarbonate.

To operate in such a challenging environment, we differentiate through our business model, which is to be a solutions provider. We focus on delivering innovative and sustainable solutions to help our customers solving complex material challenges.

*Can we consider your business « homogenous »?*

Trinseo operates on very diverse business segments and markets. And within each business, we serve a variety of customers who have different needs. Let's take two examples to illustrate this diversity.

For the consumer electronic segment, we are developing unique resin compounds that match our customers' application specific needs. Our value proposition is to be a solutions provider, supporting customers during the development of the product and then ensuring continuity of supply. Innovation, speed and flexibility are the key success factors.

On the other hand, when supplying polystyrene for the food packaging industry, quality is a given, but price is the main driver.

## What is the scope of SCM?

We have five global business units and one global supply chain organisation. Due to the nature of each business (fully global or mostly regional), we have a hybrid organisation with regional leaders running supply chain operations and global experts driving excellence in each function.

When economically relevant because of critical mass, we favour dedicated SC teams overseeing the E2E value chain. When expertise prevails –e.g. in customs and international trade compliance, resources are shared across all businesses.

Fundamentally, supply chain management is looking into the end-to-end value chain, from suppliers to customers, but this doesn't necessarily mean that all functions report hierarchically into supply chain.

## What are the main business value SCM has to provide to Trinseo competitiveness?

We have defined four domains:

- **Value Creation:** SCM fundamental mission is to support business growth and financial targets (cost and cash).
- **Customer Centricity:** delivering a superior customer experience, as part of the value proposition of each business is a fundamental attribute of SCM.
- **Operational excellence:** first imperative is to clearly define which SC model(s) is relevant to each business/segment. Then, supply chain role is to execute these models to perfection. Our credo is that supply chain connects excellence across the whole value chain.
- **Innovation:** in a fast-changing world, we constantly need to adapt and reinvent ourselves, leveraging from technology and adjusting our value proposition to remain competitive.

**What are the main actions SC has decided to perform?**

We always need to find a balance between projects that will deliver results in the short term and building long-term capabilities that require more time and effort but deliver more value over time. For 2020, our portfolio of initiatives are built around fixing value leakages (for example reducing rush shipments), improvements projects (e.g. inventory optimisation) and process streamlining and transformation projects, such as integrated business planning or supply chain segmentation.

We are now using Trinseo's newly created business excellence framework to drive excellence in supply chain and turning strategy into action.

## Take-away for leaders

The end-to-end supply chain cost represents a big part of the OPEX. Most advanced companies:

- Measure the E2E SC cost through a streamlined and integrated cost control model, potentially connected to a full chain margin approach.

- Focus on the cost-to-serve as the biggest part of the E2E SC cost by measuring it by order or/and by piece or/and by distribution channel in order to evaluate the gross margin according to the type of product, customer and distribution channel.

E2E SC cost is a major topic at the interface between all key players (purchasing, production, marketing and sales) and supply chain management, as we will analyse more comprehensively in Chapter 7. Finance has a key role to play and the recommendation is to have dedicated financial controllers and analysts in the supply chain organisation.

The E2E SC cost drivers have to be systematically analysed within elasticity studies through what-if scenarios by evaluating their impact on the product gross margin (see Chapter 13).

## Key questions to address

1. What is the degree of proximity between finance and supply chain teams?
2. How is the supply chain team involved in the procurement, production, marketing and sales decisions from an OPEX perspective?
3. Do you have a measurement of the cost-to-serve? At which level of detail is it done?
4. Have you developed a financial analysis of the customer offer and its end-to-end supply chain cost?
5. Have you implemented trainings in finance for the supply chain management community?
6. Have you implemented trainings in supply chain management for financial managers?
7. Have you appointed financial analysts in the supply chain management team?

# Chapter 4
# Generate cash

## Key ideas

### 1. The components of the cash-to-cash cycle

Three major cash flows based on the operating cycle of any company are generated by three de-synchronisations:

- Incoming raw materials and trade goods flow supplied from vendors and outgoing finished goods flow to customers. This first de-synchronisation of those flows including the work-in-progress flows in the production facilities generates inventories measured by the DIO (days of inventories outstanding).
- The second one is the result of the time from the sales to the customers and their payment, and is measured by the DSO (days of sales outstanding).
- The third one is the result of the time the company takes to pay its vendors and is measured by the DPO (days of purchasing outstanding).

The first two cash flows generate a working capital requirement and the third one generates a positive cash flow reducing this working capital requirement. Any change in the working capital requirement affects cash. Free cash flow is the net flow of liquidity that a company can generate from its business, after deducting non-operating expenses, interest, taxes, investments to maintain plants and outlets, and the change in the working capital requirement. Recently, a large company decided to launch a worldwide initiative called 'No cash no game' in order to get the commitment of all players of their value chain to play the right game to keep the free cash flow as high as possible, especially to finance growth, CAPEX and even crisis.

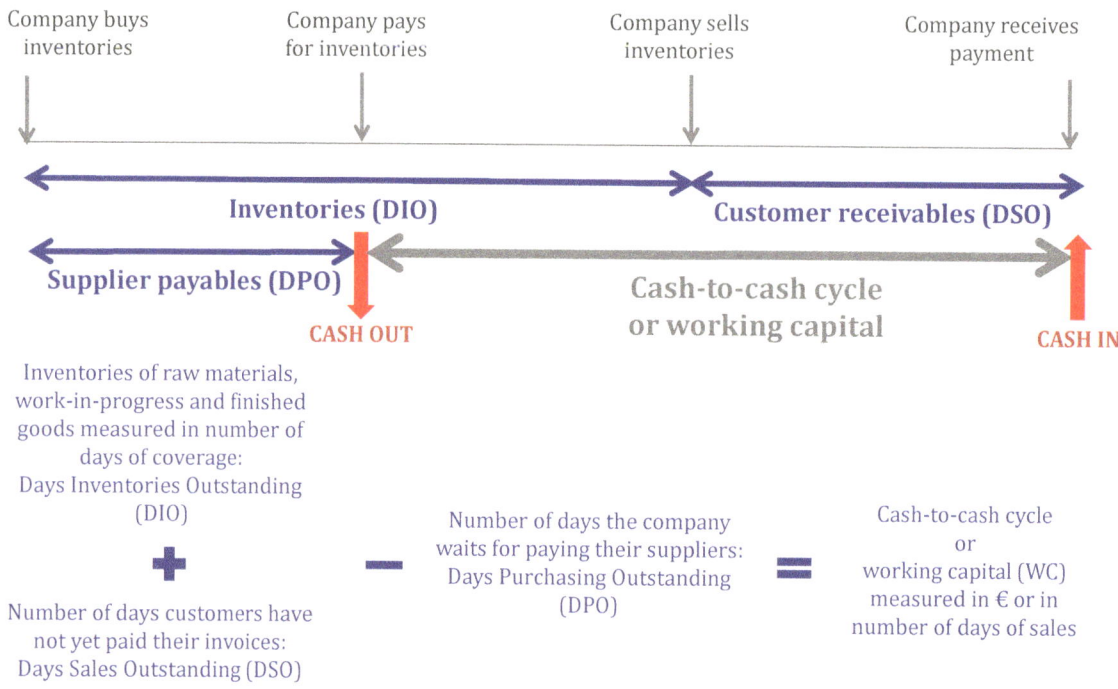

Diag.1: The components of the cash-to-cash cycle

SCM affects the three components of the cash-to-cash cycle:

- As we discussed in the Part A introduction, inventories are everywhere in the supply chains. As such, we recommend supply chain managers be accountable for inventory management. We will focus a big part of this chapter on it.
- In some companies, supply chain managers are not only accountable for order-to-delivery lead-time, explained in the Chapter 2, but for order-to-cash lead-time as well.
- The supply-to-cash lead-time depends on the vendor's portfolio and how the replenishment process is managed.

## 2. The main components of the inventories

Inventories are always the consequence of management decisions or organisation practices. Analysing them consists of detecting those underlying known or unknown, formalised or non-formalised rules and identifying which player has generated those inventories.

We differentiate generally four types of inventories, which can be applied to the different categories of stock, i.e. raw materials, work-in-progress, finished goods:

- The **safety stock**, which has the purpose to prevent and to mitigate the risk of shortage due to an extra demand, an underestimated demand forecast, a production shutdown of a supplier or of an in-house plan or quality issue. The safety stock is fundamentally linked to an uncertain event. The mathematical model dimensioning the safety stock is based on past statistical data or on predictive data estimating the probability of such risk occurrence. Keep in mind those statistical models don't follow 'normal' laws (Gauss model) as the events can occur two or three times a year only.

Even if actions can improve, for instance, quality control, demand forecast errors and production process control, volatility and uncertainty could be mitigated by a safety stock according to the most critical consequences of such events. Then, a Pareto analysis of the most critical factors of risks has to be done and the appropriate safety stocks have to be dimensioned. The most frequent risks covered by safety stocks are:

- The demand volatility.
- The demand forecast error for make-to-forecast products.
- The production reliability.
- The supplier's reliability, especially in the case of single source.

To make a good decision in terms of safety stock size, a systematic financial comparison has to be done in terms of holding inventory cost vs the value generated by this stock (extra revenue, production capacity use, etc.).

- The **cycle stock** is the consequence of the frequency of supply or production. The more frequently a product is supplied or produced, the lower the stock is. This is the principle of 'just-in-time' implemented in the Toyota Production System. The problem is that a high frequency of supply leads to half-full trucks and extra transportation costs, and a high frequency of production leads to frequent changeover of tools and a lack of the full capacity use. Therefore, a cycle stock can contribute to the saturation of the logistics means and the production capacity smoothing.

These first two stocks are interdependent. The cycle stock depends on the frequency of supply or production. Between two supplies or two production launches, there is a lead-time. This lead-time is itself a driver of the safety stock: the longer this lead-time is (the lower the frequency is), the higher the risk of shortage is, and then the higher the safety stock has to be. Stock management is a complex domain.

- The **seasonal stock** is the consequence of a seasonal inbound flow (production of raw materials such as food) and/or of a seasonal outbound flow (peak demand season). As, in general, the production capacity is flat over the year and not flexible enough in volume to face the peak season, anticipating the season by building up a seasonal stock is an answer based on the comparison of the cumulative demand pattern vs the cumulative production pattern.
- Compared to the previous three types of stocks, the **obsolete stock** is not a voluntary stock but the consequences of the slow mover products with no sales over the last months. We will have a specific analysis of that stock category in Part B, as those products have to be particularly tracked.

Other stocks, such speculative, regulatory and strategic, exist but are more specific.

## 3. The notion of healthy inventory

A good pragmatic approach to monitoring inventories is to define at the SKU level the healthy inventory as showed in diagram 2, consisting of:

- Calculating the theoretical level of the safety stock.
- Defining the minimum level of stock as 50% of the safety stock.
- Defining the maximum level as 50% above the safety stock + the batch size as the result of the frequency of supply or production + the seasonal stock.
- Following four status of the stock level:

  - Green: the stock level is healthy.
  - Red: some stock left but under the min level.
  - Black: out of stock.
  - Orange: above the stock max.

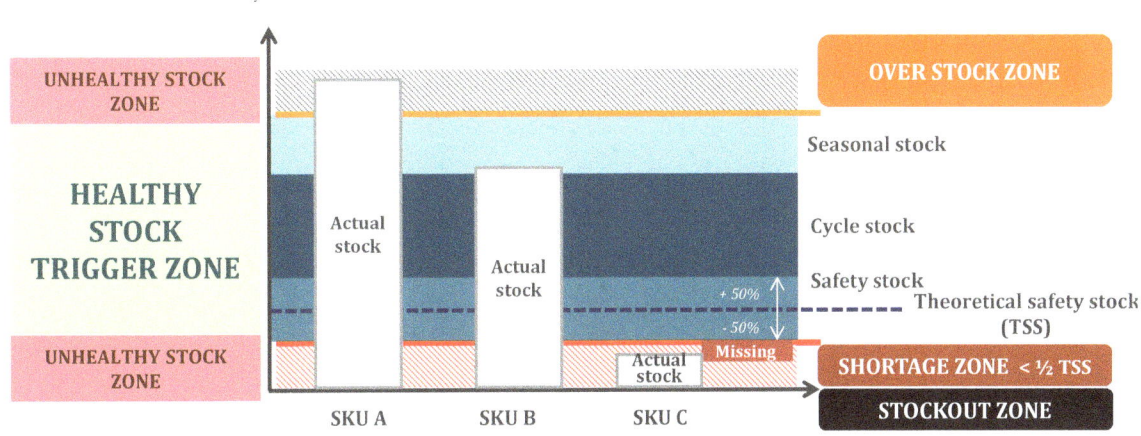

Diag.2: The definition of healthy inventory

This tool enables on a daily basis a supply manager or a production planner to make relevant decisions in terms of replenishment or production launch. The beauty of this tool is not to define a unique stock target but a green corridor, which provides some flexibility according especially to the availability of capacity and the forecasted demand.

## 4. The double financial impact of inventory

The most well-known financial impact of stock is the cash one, which impacts the working capital in the balance sheet. The second impact is the holding inventory cost, which is the cost of holding a stock over a year. This cost is evaluated as the cash multiplied by the yearly holding rate, which has four components:

- Physical: warehousing cost; insurance for both building and good; packing cost.
- Financial: the money cost rate you pay to the financial institution, which subsidises the inventories.
- Obsolescence: marketing (new product introduction replacing old product generation) and technical (shelf life) obsolescence can lead to scrap, which attacks the bottom line of the P&L.
- Shrinkage: two origins cause shrinkage: damage through handlings and theft of products.

## Take-away for leaders

The first starting point related to inventories is to measure and to control them. Appropriate KPIs have to be implemented (see Chapter 11) including the stock record accuracy. The second is to analyse the parameters of each type of stock (safety, cycle, seasonal and obsolete) and their drivers. The bad news is this work has to be done at the SKU level. The good news is that new analytical tools enable us to efficiently do that job (see introduction to Part B).

Inventories are necessary for business and generate value especially by:

- Avoiding out of stock and dissatisfying customers: the value is to provide the promised value.
- Smoothing production thanks to batch size: the value is the best use of production capacity, the limitation of CAPEX and the Return of Investment.
- Reducing the transportation cost by saturating truck or container capacity: the value is OPEX reduction.

But, those values are counterbalanced by the consumption of cash. In other words, this investment of cash should provide value to the business. If not, this is a waste. Inventory management is a typical cross-functional topic involving multiple players. Then, the optimal level of stock has to be defined.

For that purpose, our recommendation is to create a stock doctrine defining the types of stock the company has to build up to generate business value. A stock doctrine includes:

- The governance; i.e. the accountability rules related to the stock drivers and the accountable players within the organisation, especially at the central vs local levels for validating the stock parameters.
- The process of monitoring and controlling them.
- The mathematical models supporting analysis and dimensioning.

Within this stock doctrine, we recommend using the model of healthy stock based on a min/max definition.

## Key questions to address

1. Which specific KPIs have you implemented to analyse, follow and monitor your inventories?
2. Do you have a KPI measuring the stock record accuracy?
3. Have you a clear rule of stock obsolescence management? What are the solutions you have implemented to eliminate obsolescence?
4. Are you able to differentiate the different types of stocks, i.e. safety, cycle and seasonal?
5. Have you defined the dimensioning rules of each of the stock types?
6. How are the executive committee members involved in the safety stock definition?
7. Have you defined a model to simulate the service level offered to customers and the safety stock level?
8. Have you defined a model to simulate the overall production cost and the cycle stock level?
9. How is finance involved in the stock level definition?
10. Is the stock review systematically included in the agenda of the management team meeting?

# Chapter 5

# Maximise the operational and the financial value of your assets

## Key ideas make on

The contribution of SCM for generating value related to assets involves three levels of decision and planning:

## 1. The strategic planning

We consider this level of decision as it implies CAPEX decisions, and we have selected four types of decision SCM can help by preparing scenarios based on quantitative and financial models:

- The **make or buy** decision based on an analysis of core vs non-core activities along the value chain is a major driver as explained in the supply chain design. The more fragmented the value chain is, the higher number of interfaces is created. Therefore, the value chain management requires a supply chain management to monitor its internal and external players. A more integrated value chain will drive to emphasise the collaboration between the internal players.

The following diagram illustrates a differentiated make on buy strategy according to a strategic segmentation analysis. Here we have 3 segments.

- The "originals", which competes in the commodity market.
- The "trading", which enables to complete the product range offer.
- The "high performance", based on in house integration capability and which enables to generate a high margin.

| | Design | Engineer | Buy | Produce | Test | Control | Sell |
|---|---|---|---|---|---|---|---|
| The originals | | Production process engineering | Systems | Series | | Pre, WIP and post production | BUs |
| Trading | | | Finished goods buy-to-stock | | | | BUs |
| High performance | Design-to-order of special systems | Production process engineering | Systems | Production by batch | Raw materials test | Quality control in lab test | BUs |

Diag.1: Core Vs outsource, make or buy (illustration from construction products industry)

- The **footprint design** is a major and complex decision, which has a lot of supply chain management consequences and as the make or buy decision has an impact on the supply chain design. The further away the facilities are located, the more expensive the logistics costs are and the longer the lead-time is. In order to get the benefits of low resources costs (labour, raw materials, energy), many companies decided to off-shore their production facilities or their sourcing. The consequence is that worldwide geographical points have to be monitored and connected by supply chain managers.

As mentioned in the introduction of Part A, the Covid-19 crisis has highlighted the impact of the SC footprint on both agility and resilience. Some supply chains are now elligible to move down from a global-to-local to a local-to-local model.

Part A  Use SCM to generate business value

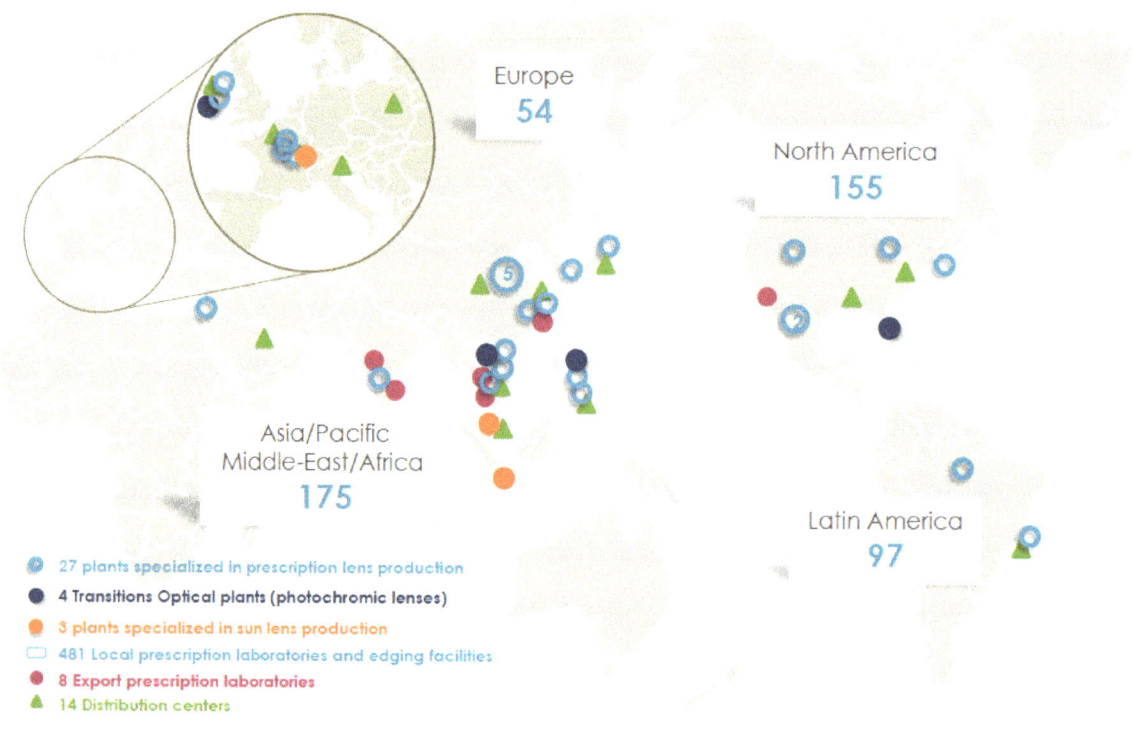

Diag.2: The footprint design (Essilor, 2019)

- The **ramp up and ramp down** leads to capacity CAPEX decision. In growing business so far (aircraft, luxury, organic food, online, etc.) this a major decision. If the capacity investment is late, there is a risk of missing the market. A good anticipation is key and a long-range planning exercise can be facilitated by SCM.

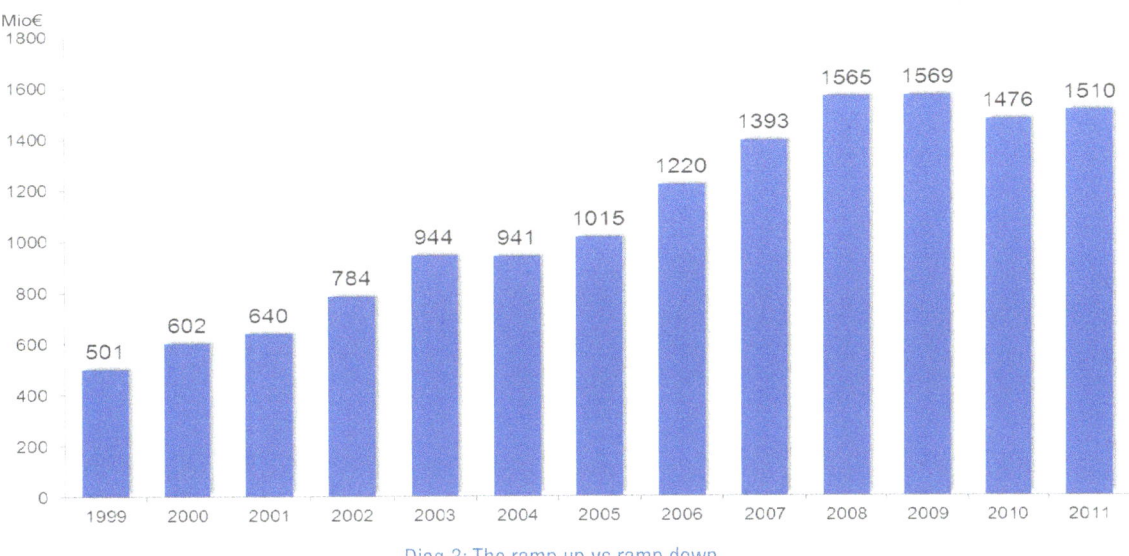
Diag.3: The ramp up vs ramp down

- The **specialisation** of the production and logistics facilities within a production and logistics network based on a given footprint has been a major driver for increasing the efficiency and the productivity of those facilities through economies of scale. All companies have successfully applied this principle, which has implied a shift from a local-to-local supply chain model to a global-to-local one. The consequence, as we can see on diagram 1, is the proliferation of the flows to connect those specialised facilities and the development of logistics facilities (warehouses, distribution centres, hubs, etc.) in order to build up the full range of products at the country level. This local product assortment enables us to deliver the full offer of products to customers with an acceptable delivery lead-time. It is clear that under the pressure on production cost, the supply chain model becomes more complex, and then the logistics cost much higher.

This strategic level of supply chain planning impacting assets return is particularly essential to consider, when the company growth is mostly based on M&A (Mergers and Aquisitions). SCM is a key success factor of M&A by evaluating its impact on the SC model, on the available capacity management and the end-to-end SC cost.

Part A  Use SCM to generate business value

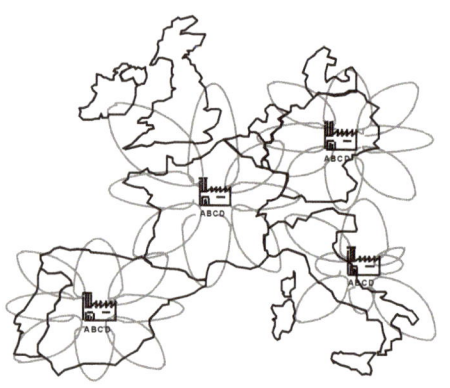
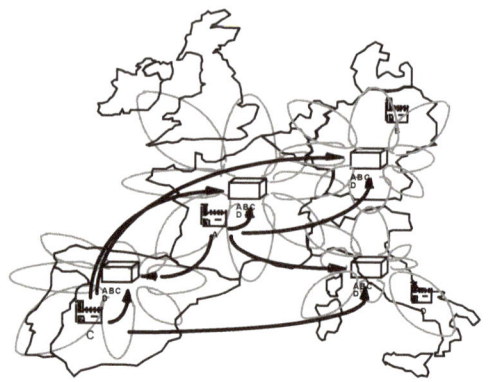

**Multi-items factories working at local level and producing full range of products (A,B,C,D)**

**Focused factories producing at international level only one specific item**

Diag.4: The production specialisation impacts on the supply chain

Those above examples show that SCM has to be involved in the elaboration of sourcing, production and marketing strategies, which are planned for at least a few years.

## 2. The tactical planning

The tactical level of decisions, which potentially impacts the return of the investments over a planning horizon of 18 to 24 months, is probably the most valuable level of supply chain planning. As we will explain (see Chapter 13), the backbone of supply chain management activities through planning is the S&OP or IBP. The first purpose of this cross-functional process is to match supply with demand and to reconcile them in order to meet the fulfilment promise to customers and to get the lowest E2E supply chain cost.

We have selected the two following topics to illustrate this value:

- According to the previous strategic decisions related to the production and logistics assets, the growth of the globalisation of supply chains generated a disconnection of the supply side from the demand side. Therefore, there is a need for deciding:
  • Which production site will be in charge of producing the demand? This decision process is called **routing** and **dispatching** or **allocation of demand** to the sources of production. This process is based on routing rules, which formalise Route-to-Markets (RTM) connecting the supply side to the demand side.

- When will this production will be done according to the available capacity and the demand pattern? This is a question of **capacity management** with the purpose of smoothing this capacity even if, as seen in Chapter 4, that generates a seasonal inventory. We call it balancing production capacity and demand. This type of decision done within the S&OP process is a typical SCM activity.

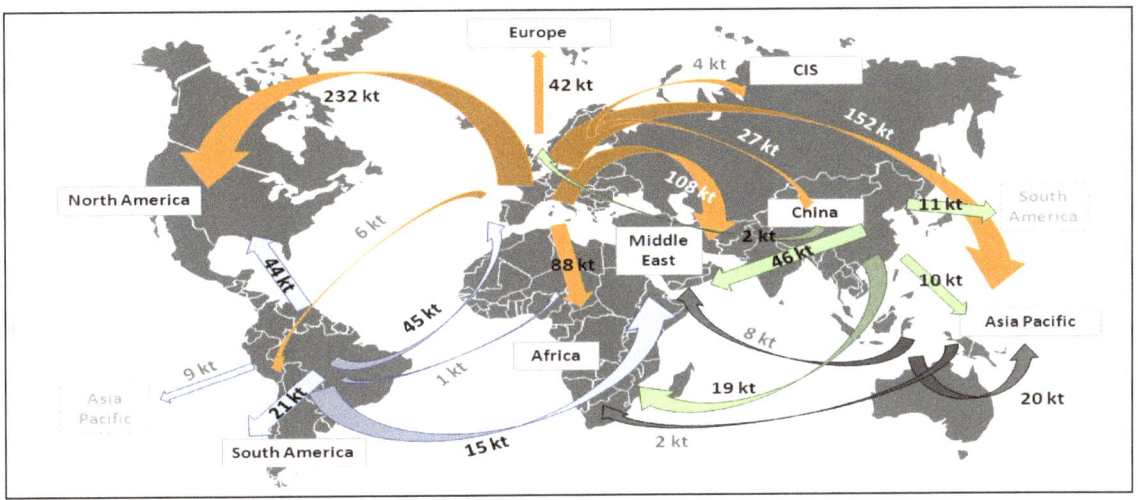

Diag.5: Allocation of demand to supply and balance demand to capacity according to the production footprint
(example from a manufacturing company in the steel industry)

– A typical situation reinforcing this role is the **seasonality** of the supply and/or the demand. Therefore, balancing supply and demand requires planning supply chain, which defines solutions to face the peak season such as the build-up of a seasonal stock, the call for subcontracting or for investing in an extra capacity.

## 3. The operational planning

The main operational decision impacting the asset value over the coming weeks is related to the operational planning of supply and production around two key questions:

- When should we launch the production of a given product?
- How much should we produce in the same batch?

Those two questions are related to the frequency of replenishment and production (see Chapter 2) and the batch size. Both impact:

- The use of **asset capacity**: as diagram 6 shows, when a machine is stopped to change over a new tool to produce another SKU, the capacity is not used and impacts negatively the **OEE** (Overall Equipment Efficiency), which is the major KPI for assessing how the invested production capacity is used or not. This changeover of tool means lack of capacity use, longer lead-time including quality stabilisation and cost. Of course, solutions exist to speed up the set-up time but they require higher flexibility of the equipment, that means additional CAPEX and this decision has to move up to the strategic planning level.
- The stock generated by the batch size (see Chapter 4), which is called a **cycle stock** due to its relationship with the frequency.

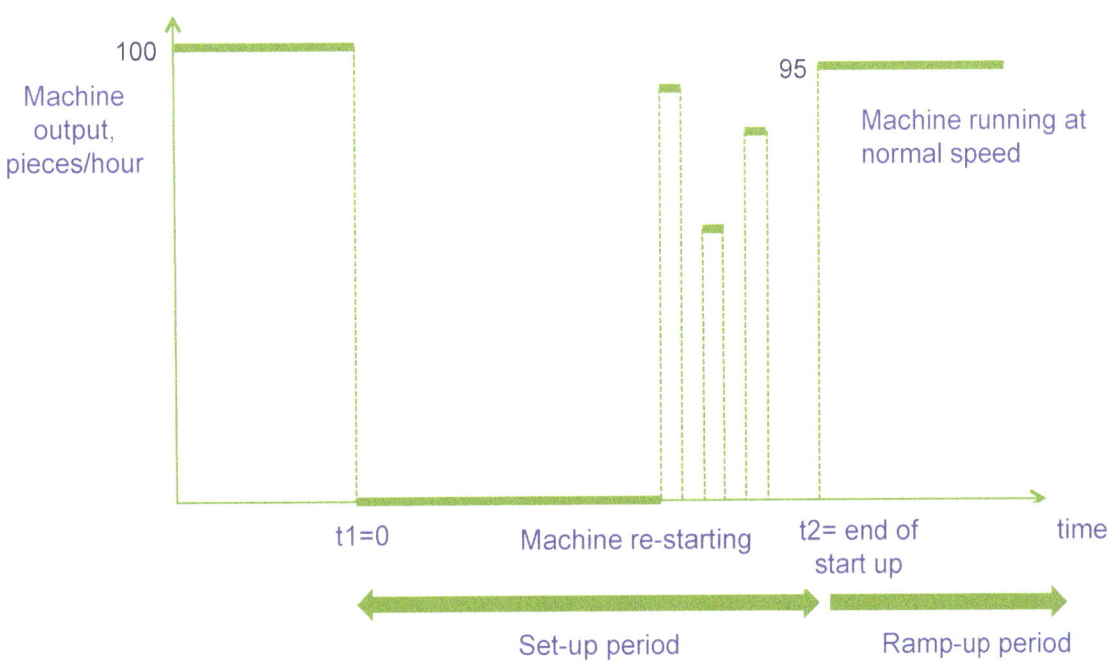

Diag.6: Overall Equipment Efficiency and level of flexibility

Due to the interdependency of the decision variables (capacity, cost, lead-time, cash), SCM is the right lens to build up a good decision.

# Testimony from Saint-Gobain Glass

Patrick DUPIN, CEO Northern Europe, Saint-Gobain, since October 2018, Former CEO Saint-Gobain Glass.

Nicolas MONDY, International Supply Chain Director since 2015, Managing Director Saint-Gobain Glass International since 2020.

Philippe BOUTONNET, Streamline and World Class Supply Chain Director since October 2019, Saint-Gobain. Former World Class Supply Chain Champion, Saint-Gobain Glass.

*What are the main challenges of your business?*

Flat glass business is a capitalistic and cyclic activity fully connected with offer and demand. Too much available capacity leads automatically to price decreases. All is emphasised by the float glass production process constraints: big investments (80M€) for big quantities, long lifetime (15 to 20 years before cold repair) and continuous fixed output from 500 to 900 tons per day.

In such a business environment, capacity management is key: making the good investment decision at the right time and the right place as well as optimising the way this capacity is used.

Success is linked to a strong cost-base model (raw material, energy, industrial performance) and to a targeted sales strategy (added value products, market segmentation, strategic customers, differentiation, customer satisfaction and intimacy, service).

Robustness of the player is demonstrated by their capacity to resist the market cycles with an adapted capacity allocation and an appropriate customer portfolio.

*How supply chain can contribute to the success of the business?*

The key role of the supply chain is to create the conditions of the collaboration between the internal functions and between the connected entities in order to develop a 'One Team' organisation aligned around a common value roadmap. Always looking to the 'general' interest of the company, sometimes against local or individual targets. The profitability of one entity often depends on the contribution of another one. In such cases, the common success requires the appropriate collaboration, trust and general guidance at global level.

A big challenge is to 'educate': develop an internal culture of supply chain management and convince the top management on its value creation based on arbitration rules. A 'global' trade-off should enable adjustments of production to key customers' satisfaction and adjustments of sales to costly production constraints.

Supply chain has the advantage to deal with very operational topics, being completely integrated into the day-to-day business between sales and production.

*You are engaged to a supply chain transformation plan since 2016: what are its main components?*

The first priority was to formalise our service charters by involving both sales and production and to improve the customers' satisfaction while developing the customer centricity within our end-to-end supply chain. A specific action plan has been rolled out to upgrade the customer service entities.

The second priority was related to the development of collaborative processes such as the reinforcement of our S&OP and the design and implementation of a stock doctrine to support top management cash objectives.

A third step (pending) consists of taking advantage of this alignment on processes and trade-offs and to propose a supply chain segmentation and allow a service offer differentiation by product families or by markets.

All those actions have been with the double ambition of empowering the local players such as production planning, customer service, and developing global standards animated by the central supply chain team.

*What are the outcomes of that program and the learnt lessons?*

The role of the Saint-Gobain Glass supply chain has clearly evolved in the past years from a 'logistics' support function to a key player in the company with profitability creation. A key success factor was the contribution of top management who involved supply chain in most of the strategic decisions whenever it could contribute.

Sales team adhesion to the transformation program was motivated by their expectations to improve service to their customers. Trade-offs on sales allocations as well as customer promises definition have been understood and accepted as a necessary business contribution.

The production teams have also adapted their day-to-day attitude by matching better with market demand as demonstrated by a +10% OTIF score in 3 years.

Marketing have launched initiatives to better understand customer needs and service differentiation requests. This process is still pending as well as product range definition to enable an appropriate supply chain segmentation.

*What are the next steps?*

The market is changing and the strategy of Saint-Gobain Glass is evolving. Supply chain has to adapt its priorities to the business strategy and the Saint-Gobain 'Transform & Grow' 2019 organisation initiative. The main topics are the following:

- Added value products and key customers remain a priority in terms of service and growth.

- Cost-to-serve for commodities has to be analysed at every step of the supply chain from sand to glazing. This includes taking the benefits of the investments done in IT tools.

- Stocks connected to cash availability are crucial and has to become a driver of the business and not just a consequence.

## Take-away for leaders

It is clear that SCM is not accountable for making decisions related to make or buy strategy, footprint evolution, capacity CAPEX for structural ramp up volume based on organic growth or M&A, or for managing a seasonal demand pattern, but SCM is definitely the right lens to facilitate the elaboration of scenarios based on quantitative and financial models.

Those decisions are related to three complementary levels, which impact the assets value, strategic, tactical and operational. As we will see in Chapter 13, SCM has to play a fundamental role in connecting the multiple players to involve in such highly interdependent and multi-dimensional decision variables and then, to facilitate the emergence of a common decision based on a collaborative planning process.

Those asset-based decisions are dependant on the previous value pillars we analysed in the previous chapters and will lead to the first paradigm of SCM exposed in Chapter 7.

## Key questions to address

1. Do you involve supply chain managers in the sourcing, production and marketing strategies formulation?
2. Have you formalised specific processes to support your decisions at the three complementary levels, i.e. strategic, tactical and operational?
3. Have you included ROI in your supply chain models?
4. Do you involve your SC manager in your M&A activities?
5. Have you designed and formalised Route-to-Markets from the sourcing points to the customers delivery points?
6. Have you simulated the CAPEX required for a higher equipment flexibility vs the cash impact of higher cycle stock?
7. Have you implemented a monthly tactical process such as S&OP or IBP to reconcile capacity and demand simulating OPEX and cash impacts?

# Chapter 6
# Focus on sustainable and resilient supply chains

## Key ideas

The sustainability framework is made of the pillars named the 3Ps, as follows:

**PEOPLE**
- Safe and ergonomic solutions based on 4.0
- One Team based on a shared leadership
- Respect of social regulations
- Sustainable organisations

**PLANET**
- $CO_2$ emissions and carbon footprint
- Digital solutions for logistics flow optimisation
- Circular economy and recycling waste
- Concurrent and modular product design

**PROFIT**
- Long term financials
- Risks mitigation along the full end-to-end supply chain and resilient organisations
- Business continuity plan

Diag.1: The three pillars of sustainability

– The **People**: as we explained in the Part A introduction all players of a value chain belong to a supply chain and one of the missions of supply chain managers is to connect those players through collaborative processes for the general interest of the company.

Several dimensions are related to people as follows:

- The first value that any company has to work on is to ensure a **safe** work environment to its employees. In supply chain many logistics and production operations are performed. The application and the respect of safety rules in any place of work are the first value promoted by any company. A 4.0 approach can provide relevant solutions, which can be coupled with a better ergonomic for better health.
- SCM is the most cross-functional process of any company and its first purpose is to build up **One Team** aligned around a common value roadmap. We will see in the next chapter how the first paradigm of SCM enables us to strengthen this fundamental notion of One Team.
- Sourcing and production footprint decisions can lead to some regions in the world where the **social regulations** have not the same standard as in the mother country of the company. This is key to make sure those regulations are respected as a global standard.
- Once, a supply chain director told me that his highest mission is to make people happy around him and to manage the **stress**. Stress is like cholesterol, you have bad stress and good stress. A rush order, a back-order, a stock out situation, a cash issue, a natural catastrophe, a strike and so many potential events will generate a high level of stress. The role of supply chain managers is to keep cool and to find out solutions to support people in their own job. Former military officers can be very good supply chain officers.

– The **planet**: the carbon footprint of any supply chain is potentially huge with gas and energy consumption and $CO_2$ emissions, though not limited to these. This is the overwater part of the iceberg and we would like to highlight at least the three following topics:

- The main driver of the **carbon footprint** related to supply chain is the supply chain model itself, as explained in the Part A introduction, i.e. its level of fragmentation and globalisation. 4.0 innovations enable logistics flows

optimisation by saturating the transportation means, especially thanks to round trips. Those innovations are related for instance to smart automation, predictive maintenance, supply chain network design optimisation, transportation management systems and real time tracking of flows.
- Beyond that, the lack of integration/collaboration between product designer, production process designer and supply model designer leads to a high impact on the planet. IKEA is one of the historical companies that has put in its DNA this **eco-friendly supply chain model** design based on a strong collaboration between the main supply chain players. There is a huge opportunity of value creation by co-working on product design and on supply chain model.
- The third topic, which is related to the previous one, is the **circular economy** and more specifically the returns of goods, waste management and recycling of used goods. A major stake is the development of closed loops of flows in and out using the same transportation facilities to have full capacity of those facilities in round trips. This type of innovative solution is enabled by new digital solutions.

– The **Profit**: the last pillar of sustainability concerns the long-term resilience of the company, which is based on its profit and the free cash flow generation to invest in its future. Mitigating the potential **supply chain risks,** which could jeopardise the revenue generation, is a key mission of supply chain management to develop business continuity plans. Strikes, floods, fires, earthquakes and international health issues like Covid-19 are probable events that can break down the supply chain at a local or a global level. We highly recommend valuing the risks in the mathematical models used for testing SC models.

## Take-away for leaders

We believe that sustainability should belong to the value roadmap of any company. Even if sustainability is not selected as a strategic priority, some actions seem to be compulsory for any company to support this long-term value. The three pillars of sustainability concern in priority firstly the major asset, people, then the ecosystem and the external environment where the company develops itself, and finally the endogen sustainability of the company based on its long-term profit.

The first sustainable value that SCM can reinforce is to get One Team of people, first at the top management level and then within the full organisation, aligned around a common value roadmap. This is one of the leadership dimensions that SCM can support in order to get a sustainable organisation. Taking care of people in terms of their safety and their comfort belong to the key missions of supply chain managers. 4.0 solutions participate fully to a safe and ergonomic environment for people.

Eco-friendly supply chain solutions are probably the domain of supply chains with the highest rate of innovations. Some of these innovations include: concurrent modular design of products according to modular design of supply chains; positive energy logistics and production facilities; multi-purpose buildings enabling a reduction of urban transportation for the last mile based on outbound consolidated flows; new transportation solutions by sea and on ground; and design of round trips based on sophisticated transportation management systems.

Finally, supply chain managers will contribute to building up sustainable revenue and profit by managing potential risks and future shocks, which can break down the revenue of a company. In order to develop **the resilience of the supply chains,** the main axes are:

- The assessment of the **vulnerabilities** of the current supply chains.
- The development of **concurrent supply chain models** based on both global-to-global and local-to-local models (see introduction Part A and Chapters 10 and 12).

- The **simplification** of the supply chain model by reducing the number of steps internally (through horizontally seamless and vertically flatter organisations) and externally (fewer tiers of both suppliers and customers). This means the reduction of the fragmentation of global supply chains.
- The **acceleration of the end-to-end flows** in order to connect the supply side and the demand side more quickly.
- The **re-definition of the offers** to customers by rationalising it, if this is acceptable according to the strategic market positioning (see Chapter 10).
- The systematic development of a **second source** of supply based on diversified geography and a long-term relationship with the new suppliers.
- The implementation of **safety stocks** in a healthier manner (see Chapter 13).

## Key questions to address

1. How have you embedded sustainability in your business plan?
2. Do you consider sustainability a strategic leverage of your business?
3. Do you consider sustainability a value for your business?
4. Out of the three pillars of the sustainability model, which one have you included in your daily activities?
5. Do you use supply chain management as a leverage of the One Team dimension of your organisation in order to better sustain it?
6. Which 4.0 solutions have you implemented to increase your company sustainability for people, planet or profit?
7. Which solutions have you implemented to develop a green supply chain?
8. Is supply chain management accountable for designing business continuity plans in case of a major event?
9. Have you included the carbon footprint and the energy consumption in your mathematical supply chain models?

# Chapter 7

# Clarify your value proposition based on the first paradigm of SCM: trade-off

## Key ideas

### 1. The first paradigm of SCM: the trade-off

In the previous six chapters, we have already provided examples of contradictory objectives in terms of value creation within the five-parameter value equation. The following table shows some of the most critical topics, which illustrate contradictions between certain numbers of parameter-values:

| Parameter value involved | Topic |
|---|---|
| Service vs Cost vs Cash vs Asset vs Sustainability | Order-to-delivery lead-time |
| Service vs Cost vs Cash | Order size (delivered volume) |
| Service vs Cost vs Cash | Frequency of deliveries |
| Service vs Cash | Fulfilment rate (in full rate) |
| Service vs Cost vs Cash | Number of SKUs (product range) |
| Cost vs Cash vs Asset | Batch size (replenishment and production) |
| Cost vs Cash vs Asset | Flexibility of machinery |
| Cash vs Sustainability | Mass volume transportation solutions |

The previous list is not comprehensive and, as we can see, some contradictory values involve two values or three or even four. For instance:

- A high fulfilment rate will increase the OTIF and the value perceived by the customers, but will require a higher safety stock, which means a negative value on cash.
- Long distance transportation based on huge vessels will enable the reduction of $CO_2$ emissions but will generate a large work-in-progress inventory, impacting negatively the cash level.
- The batch size in a replenishment or in a production operation has a triple impact on the cost of change over, handling or transportation (the higher the batch is, the lower the logistics cost is), the cash (the higher the batch size is, the higher the inventory is) and the asset use (the higher the batch size, the less frequently change overs are required).
- The order-to-delivery lead-time is definitely one of the major drivers of value and has an impact on all five parameters of value with opposite impacts in terms of value creation.

Potentially, a big number of interdependent contradictory relationships are possible. The right way of fixing it is not to study all those relationships, which is by essence quite complex, but to use a process called 'trade-off' as explained in the next paragraph. We consider the trade-off as a paradigm of SCM.

## 2. The value roadmap: the role of leaders and supply chain managers

The formalisation of the value roadmap shows the three steps of the trade-off process:

- **Step 1**: the former examples highlighting the contradictions in terms of value creation make a link to the mathematical background of SCM, which is operations research. The purpose of this maths field is to apply **optimisation** algorithms to fix complex problem based on multiple variables impacting in opposite ways a value objective function under constraints, for instance of cash, or customer service or production capacity. Then, supply chain managers have to model a supply chain situation, which consider the constraints, the decision variables to study and the value objective to optimise and use solvers to find out the optimal solution. Maths people perform this step with input provided by supply chain managers.

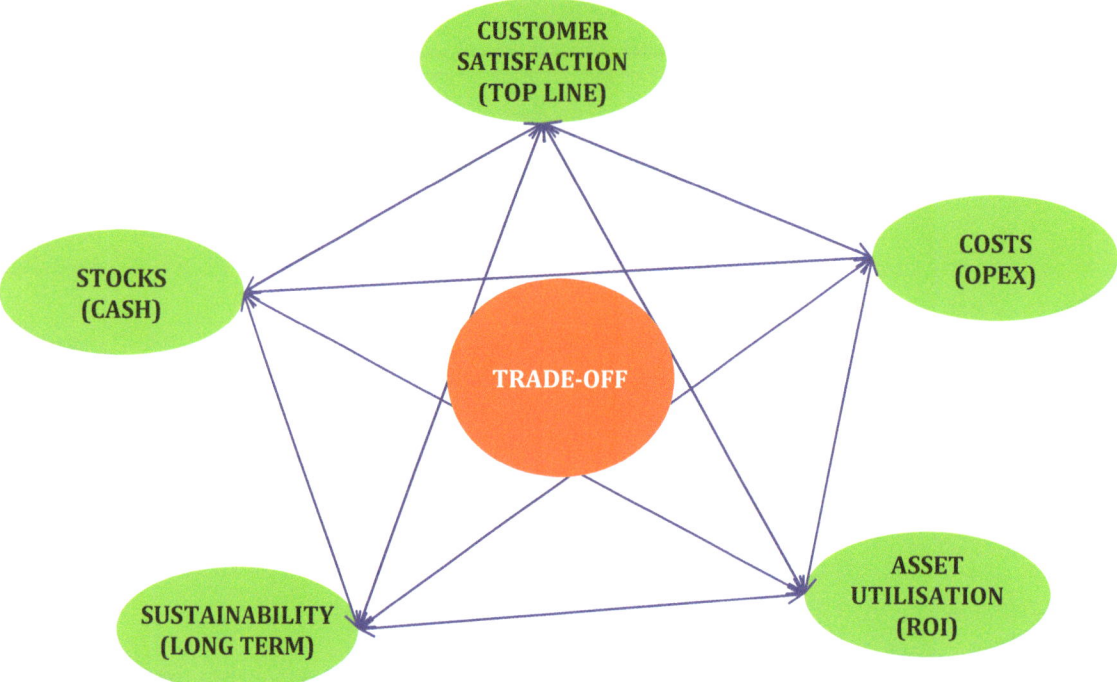

Diag.1: The multiple trade-offs between the five-parameter value equation

- **Step 2**: based on modelled situations, the supply chain managers will formalise **what-if scenarios** and propose **trade-offs** to the top management.
- **Step 3**: the role of supply chain managers is to propose scenarios and the final decision is under the top management leadership's accountability. Especially in case of conflicts between the main stakeholders, there is an escalation and the CEO will **arbitrate** and chooses one scenario according to the strategy of the company. This arbitration is the input for the value roadmap formalisation.

## 3. The value roadmap has to derive from the strategy

Diagram 2 shows practical examples of the application of the trade-off paradigms as follows:

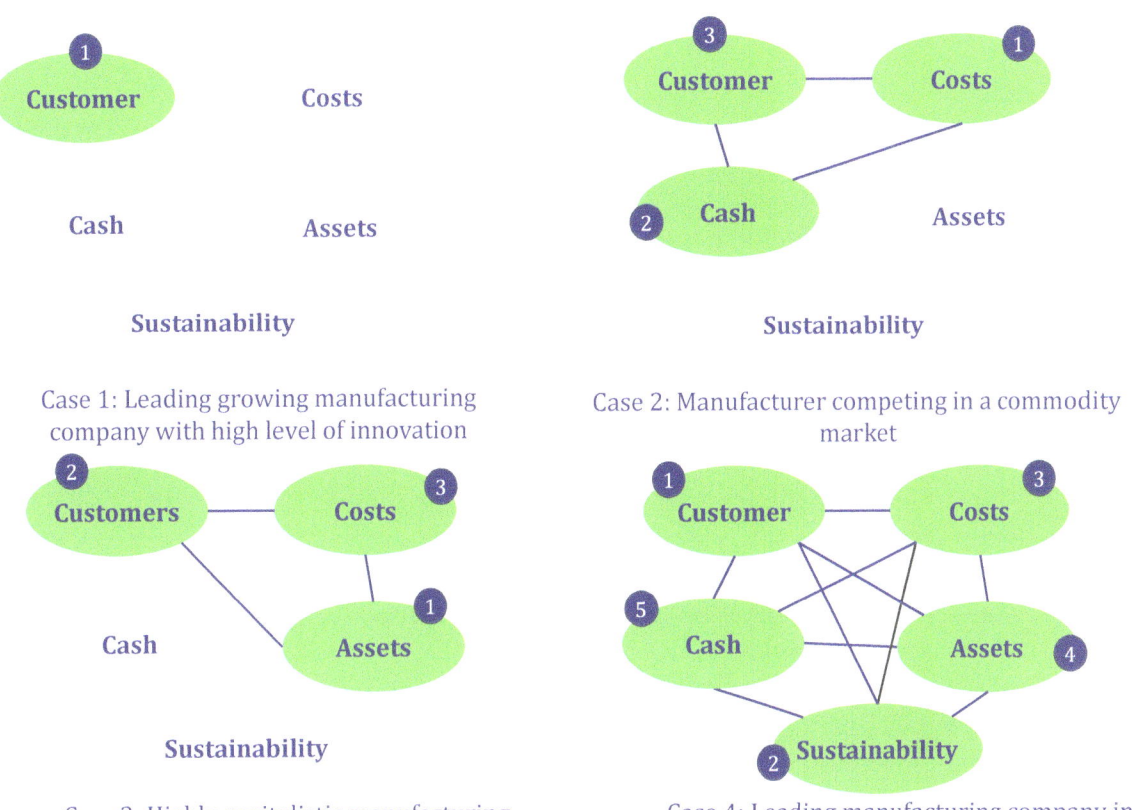

Diag.2: Examples of companies and trade-offs according to their value roadmap

- **Case 1**: high-tech companies with a strategy based on product innovation and time-to-market consider growth as the major stake. Therefore, the value roadmap will be focused primarily and essentially on the customers' satisfaction whatever the cost-to-serve and the cash consumption can be.
- **Case 2**: this company competing in a commodity market has decided to compete first on cost, then on cash and finally on customer satisfaction. This is an example of a company not putting customer satisfaction as a first priority. In this case of a fabless

company, asset use is not a priority and logistics operations are as well subcontracted to 3PL (Third Party Logistics) and as a US company under high competitive pressure, sustainability is definitely not on its agenda.
- **Case 3**: for this high capital intensive company performing in the oil and gas industry, characterised by huge CAPEX (a new plant is around 1 B$), this is clear that OEE through asset saturation is the major value that SCM can facilitate. Therefore as a second priority, customer satisfaction emerged with a stronger competition on the OTIF respect and for instance half million dollars of penalties in case of one day of delivery late. As a third priority, cost becomes a challenge under the pressure of lower cost country-based competitors.
- **Case 4**: this case is the most sophisticated example of a value roadmap based on the five parameters. For this manufacturing company performing in the dairy industry:

  - Customer satisfaction is the first priority;
  - Sustainability is the second consistently with the strategic market positioning of health for people;
  - Cost-to-serve is the third due to the pressure of the private labels of the retailers, which are actually the first customer of that company as well their first competitor;
  - Asset use optimisation is the fourth according to the low margin of that industry;
  - Cash is the last value objective, which is quite consistent with an industry characterised of product shelf life of twelve days. This is a Just-in-Time industry, which has developed a quite fast end-to-end supply chain lead-time.

The fundamental take-away of those examples is that the value roadmap has to be built up according to the strategic priorities of the company.

# Testimony from Nespresso

Jean-Michel CECCONI, Director of Innovation, Nespresso France.

Stefano BARISZA, Head of Operations, Nespresso France.

*What are the pillars of the Nespresso business ambition?*

The ambition of Nespresso since its launch in Switzerland in 1986 is to offer the best coffee day after day. To carry this ambition, Nespresso relies on three pillars: coffee, machines, and service to our members.

To achieve this goal, Nespresso has created an extensive quality-sourcing program directly from selected farmers through the Nespresso AAA program. A complete system has been developed using aluminium capsules to protect the quality of the coffee combined with high-pressure extraction machines.

To better serve Nespresso consumers, several logistics organisations support the various distribution channels, e-commerce, and boutiques, in B2C as well as in B2B.

*What are the main changes related to the Nespresso business model?*

Nespresso used to sell portion coffee for a long time on a closed and new market. Over the years, coffee consumption habits have changed. In 2020, the consumption of coffee in portions represents in quantity more than a third of consumption in France. The opening to competition that took place after the end of the patents accelerated the development of the Nespresso system in general. The consumer offer has become wider with increased accessibility thanks to the opening of a new distribution channel through supermarkets and hypermarkets.

*How can supply chain management serve this business ambition and the business model evolution?*

In a direct business to the consumer, the supply chain function is essential. It will deliver the promise of service made to customers. As often in these back-office functions, operation in line with the promise is considered normal, however, operation below the promise is considered unacceptable and creates consumer dissatisfaction.

The supply chain must therefore excel to meet customer expectations. Excellence is measured by reliability, quality, cost and time in the execution of flows.

In the context of a wider offer to customers and consumers and in a direct distribution model, the supply chain can contribute in several ways:

- Facilitate accessibility to products for customers by increasing the number of contact points to give the most suitable choice for each customer situation.
- Reduce the delivery time by offering a wide choice of delivery method (mailbox, pick-up relay, niche delivery).
- Guarantee a constant quality of the service with compliant deliveries.

This growth in the supply chain offer has to keep the expected level of overall excellence.

***Do you consider the link between finance and supply chain close enough? Which best practices have you developed in that perspective?***

The link between finance and supply chain is strong at the following two levels:

- The level of the company's forecasts, which is a responsibility that is also shared with marketing in order to assess future trends and to bring the expected commercial elements that will impact future trends up or down. Finally, finance will work on the consolidated and macro vision of forecasts to take into account any exogenous elements to the company and ensure consistency with the company's budget plans already shared with stakeholders (management, shareholders, analysts, etc.).
- In terms of cost management, the supply chain is a very important cost centre in a company like Nespresso. Again, a good allocation of roles is essential. The supply chain generates costs and has to work on quantitative indicators in order to improve them. Finance enhances supply chain data and ensures consistency with financial plans. If necessary, new financial objectives can be defined in collaboration with supply chain, which will break them down into quantitative sub-objectives for the teams.

*Can you explain the mission of the innovation entity within Nespresso?*

The mission of the Open Innovation hub within Nespresso is to open up to external innovation carried by start-ups but also by larger companies. Its objective is to develop innovations that will have an impact on sales growth, by exploring new territories or by evolving existing models. This relates to new business models, new routes-to-market, new marketing methods or new technologies.

External innovation is a way to open up possibilities and accelerate innovation by taking advantage of more agile operations that are difficult to implement within large organisations.

There is no contradiction between the two operating modes; they are simply best suited to their mission. Large organisations must optimise and secure as much as possible operations on their central activities. They will therefore simplify, standardise and automate. Innovation must by nature work differently with different solutions in order to hope to obtain disruptive innovation compared to existing models and thus maintain or increase a competitive advantage.

The hub tests each opportunity with pilots, the results of which are shared with the sales and marketing teams who decide to deploy at the end.

*How can supply chain management participate in this innovation ambition?*

The supply chain in a business like Nespresso is at the heart of activities. It is concerned with all areas of innovation. It can participate by being an actor in innovation projects or by bringing new ideas obtained by observing logistics partners or companies targeting the same categories of customers.

We can identify three main contributions of supply chain to business innovation, and all of them are based on technology and digital transformation and we are working on it to make them a reality. The first one is the capacity to track each step of the coffee chain from the crops to the final delivery almost in real time. In addition to the perfect traceability of our coffee, the first consequence is the possibility of sharing at any moment with the consumers the details of this journey from the origin of the coffee to the final delivery, downstream and upstream. Another consequence, more relevant in terms of service, is the real time tracking of each order; we can share with the consumer not only the status of the order (waiting time, prepared, shipped, etc.) but also the geographical position, the expected delivery time and the GPS position of the delivery. New technologies allow the easy and secure sharing of information between the players of the supply and the final customers.

A second contribution relates to automation: supply chain is an activity with a huge physical footprint. Inbound transport, finished goods storage, order preparation and parcel delivery are all activities with a significant amount in terms of investment and labour. There is no doubt that through technology it's possible to optimise investments and increase efficiency: automated unloading and loading of trucks, high-density warehouse and automatic order preparation are the main areas of automation.

The third contribution of supply chain to innovation concerns the environmental footprint. We work on several projects in collaboration with our transport partners with the aim of strongly reducing the $CO_2$ emissions: replacing the transport fleet with a new electric one especially for the last mile of delivery is only one example.

In summary, supply chain can participate to innovation in three main areas: improving customer experience, optimising investment and efficiency, reducing environmental footprint.

# Take-away for leaders

A funny way to illustrate the trade-off as the first paradigm of SCM is to say that every time we have good news generated from SCM, we have bad news. For instance, a fast delivery of an order to a customer (good news), which improves the OTIF and even the NPS, will increase the cost-to-serve (bad news). This is the same with a safety stock (bad news related to cash), which enables to meet an unexpected demand (good news). From a mathematical perspective, this is a question of optimisation. The wrong way is to trust digital tools to fix this optimisation problem. The good way is to apply a three-step process of trade-off. The following table summarises the three steps of that trade-off process:

| People accountable | Step of the process | Input | Output |
|---|---|---|---|
| Data scientists and modelling experts | Optimisation | Models and solvers | Optimal solutions |
| Supply chain managers | Trade-off | Constraints and value drivers | What-if scenarios based on trade-offs |
| CEO | Arbitration | Business plan and strategic market positioning | Value roadmap based on strategic priorities |

As we will see in Chapter 13, this paradigm is supported by the tactical S&OP/IBP process. This process is owned by the CEO and facilitated by the SCM, which is quite consistent with the previous table. The mission of SCM is to challenge top managers and to push them to clarify their value proposition. In a way, SCM is an enabler of strategic clarification and SCM is a leverage to link strategy to operations.

Part A  Use SCM to generate business value

## Key questions to address

1. Have you formalised your value proposition?
2. Have you linked your value proposition to the five-parameter value equation and formalised the potential conflicts within those five parameters?
3. Have a clear vision of your priorities in terms of value creation?
4. Do you consider that the management team (executive committee) is aligned around a common goal, i.e. a common value roadmap?
5. Have you involved supply chain managers in the arbitration process?
6. Have you a formalised escalation process in case of conflicts between players within your organisation in terms of value creation priorities?
7. Is your CEO clearly identified as the owner of arbitration in case of conflicts regarding value creation?
8. Is SCM clearly identified as the facilitator of the value roadmap elaboration and its animation?
9. Have you formalised mathematical models modelling the major value conflicts of your business?

# Chapter 8
# Financialise your supply chain management to generate value

## Key ideas

In the previous chapters, we have identified three major dimensions of SCM contribution in terms of value creation:

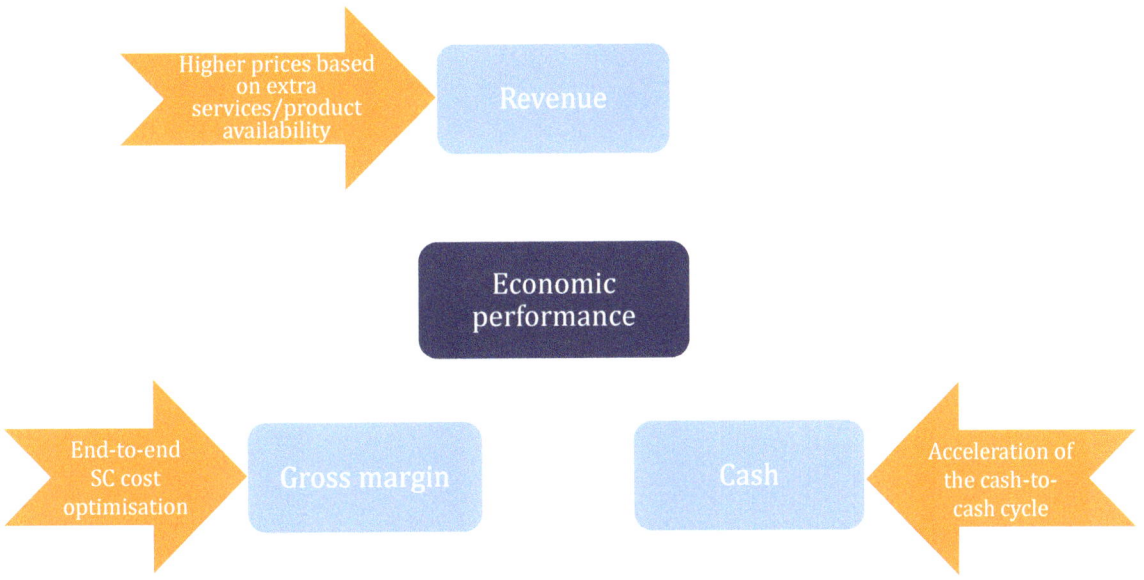

Diag.1: The major axes of the economic performance improved by SCM

- Economic value: revenue, gross margin and cash as displayed in the diagram 1.
- Social value: safety, work conditions, social regulations and aligned stakeholders.
- Environmental value: $CO_2$ emissions, energy consumption, infrastructures impacts and waste management and recycling.

Part A  Use SCM to generate business value

These value axes have a financial translation into the financial statements, i.e. the P&L and the balance sheet as listed in diagram 2:

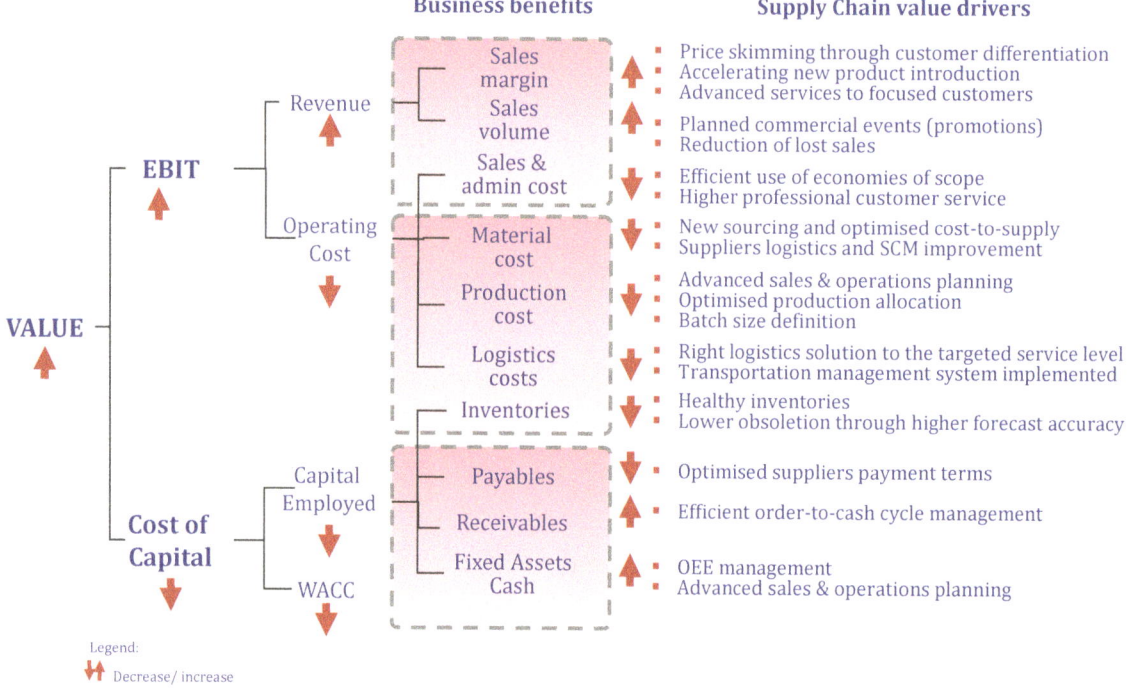

Diag.2: The financial impacts of SCM

## 1. Impacts of SCM on financial statements

### a) The impact on the P&L

The main items of the P&L impacted by SCM decisions are:

- **Top line**: the revenue is influenced by:
    - The extra price charged to the customers in case of premium services.
    - The extra volume generated by new offers of products and services and by commercial events such as promotions.
    - The elimination of lost sales in case of stock out situations.

All those benefits are possible thanks to a close collaboration between sales, marketing and SCM especially for designing offers and planning demand based on new product introduction and commercial activities.

- **Commercial gross margin:** the commercial expenses such as samples, merchandising materials and customer service (people, IT). As we mentioned the supply chain dedicated to sample can be quite expensive and customer service, which can report to the supply chain team, has to provide value to the customer beyond its routine order management activity.
- **EBITDA:** the operating expenses cover the end-to-end supply chain. Chapter 3 provided details on the components of those operating expenses and involve:
    - The sourcing done by the purchasing team and the cost-to-supply consequences.
    - The production costs according to the location of the plants and access to the main resources (people and energy).
    - The cost-to-serve related to the handling and transportation activities for delivering orders to the customers.
    - The impact of inventories has already been explained in Chapter 4. Complementary to that, the variation of inventories has an impact on the P&L, which must not be underestimated. This impact is contradictory with the positive balance sheet impact. A reduction of finished good stock is positive from the cash perspective but negative on the EBITDA.

## b) The impact on the balance sheet

The main items of the balance sheet impacted by SCM are:

- **The working capital (WC):**
    - Inventories: the impact of inventories on cash has been detailed in Chapter 3 as well as the multiple drivers of them.
    - Receivables: in some companies, the supply chain officer is not only accountable for the order-to-delivery lead-time but also the order-to-cash lead-time. The receivable lead-time is generally co-decided by sales and finance but its application and control can be delegated to SCM.
    - Payables: buyers define with finance the financial terms within the purchasing contracts with the suppliers and as for receivables, SCM can be in charge of controlling its right application through audit procedures.

- **The assets**: the level of assets for a given level of revenue depends on how the invested capacity is used. Here SCM plays a fundamental role, especially through facilitating the S&OP or the IBP (see Chapter 13). An optimal S&OP process will enable the reduction of the requirements of CAPEX.

c) The overall financial value of SCM related to cash flow

As mentioned in Chapter 4, P&L and balance sheet are connected through the generation of cash flow, which is the result of EBITDA as OCF (Operating Cash Flow) including the impact of working capital. This OCF is used for financing the CAPEX and the net result is the free cash flow (FCF) before tax.

## 2. The three levels of SCM decisions impact the financial fundamentals

A complementary approach consists of matching the SCM activities and decisions impacting the financial fundamentals of a company at three complementary levels as detailed in the following table:

| Decision level | Main SCM activities impacting the financial fundamentals |
|---|---|
| Strategic design | - Model supply chain in order to select the most appropriate ones based on the value roadmap from the five-pillar value model: top line, OPEX, cash, assets and sustainability<br>- Evaluate the financial consequences of the risks<br>- Model route-to-market for connecting the first tier of suppliers to the first tier of customers by considering<br>- Evaluate the end-to-end supply chain cost<br>- Manage the full chain margin |
| Tactical and operational monitoring | - Sales & operations planning decisions based on trade-off rules<br>- Production batch sizing<br>- Healthy inventories sizing<br>- Supply versus demand sides optimisation based on margin in order to manage the product portfolio in a limited capacity environment by evaluating:<br>  ✓ Cost-to-serve<br>  ✓ Price |
| Operational excellence | - Cost-to-serve optimisation by customer order including picking, packing, shipping |

Table 1: Financial impacts of supply chain management

# Testimony from a Wall Street Influencer

Manish A. SOMAIYA, Wall Street Influencer, Former Managing Director & Head of Credit Research, Citigroup Global Markets, Inc.

*In general, what is the competence level (or awareness level) of the financial world in the supply chain area?*

Investors' focus on the supply chain has historically comprised of a second or third derivative analysis of monitoring the company and industry. It is a by-product of analysing and forecasting financial metrics as most investors have expertise in finance and capital markets versus the intricacies of operational planning and analysis. Few sectors are immune from the impact of Covid-19, and the topic of the supply chain has gained prominence amongst investors, especially on the back of well-documented shortages of critical drugs and medicines, along with necessities such as toilet tissue. While Brexit and Sino–US trade tensions have captivated financial audiences, the shock of Covid-19 is more personal. Overall, the pandemic has crystalized just-in-time from the supply chain, and the deep connection and differences between the two topics.

*What are « historically » the major fields investors have targeted in SC?*

The top three industries attracting the most amount of capital historically are business & productivity software, automotive, and communications software. By verticals, the prime beneficiaries are supply chain tech, TMT and mobility tech, also according to Pitchbook data. Interestingly, the investments have continued to flow to these sectors at a more rapid pace in recent years. In the US, 2019 was the most active year in the past decade from investments garnered from venture capital and public markets at just over $23 billion, doubling from the year before. It was also a banner year for public investments with over $8 billion associated with UBER's IPO alone.

*What is the profile of investors investing in SC?*

Venture capital and incubator firms are the most active by deal count in the broader supply chain space, based on Pitchbook data. Silicon Valley heavyweights such as

Sequoia Capital and Kleiner Perkins and GV (formerly Google Ventures) along with accelerator firms, Y Combinator, Plug and Play Tech Center, and New Enterprise Associates have completed the greatest number of transactions. Many companies within the space experience multiple rounds of financings before showing a public exit, like Uber or Grub hub. Due to the dependency on substantial debt financing for the transaction, private equity participation is limited and hence making it more conducive for venture capital.

**What is the probable evolution in SC investments after the COVID-19?**

The Covid-19 pandemic is likely to spur investments in a host of areas, including autonomous delivery, online grocery and food delivery apps, warehousing marketplaces, and freight platforms. One must also consider the impact of forced or voluntary insourcing, a function of policy pressures or strategy on the part of companies to diversify geographic and supplier exposure. Specialty pharma, with the shortages of critical generic drugs, stands out. Factory automation is another area where global industrials can limit the impact of future market shocks. In the future, expect increased automation AI and digitisation.

## Take-away for leaders

SC especially through logistics and digital tools is a key domain of large investments stimulated by innovation. Both P&L and balance sheet in their most critical items are potentially impacted positively by an advanced way of managing the supply chain: top line, gross margin, EBITDA for the P&L, working capital, cash and fixed assets for the balance sheet. As a result, the benefits concern both the free cash flow (FCF) and the weighted average cost of capital (WACC).

Up to now, most supply chain management teams are poor in terms of finance and even the S&OP process has been run with technical units and not financial ones. Then, a key axis of SCM team development is to include financial analysts and controllers in order to financialise the supply chain models and to value the SCM benefits. Supply chain and financial managers talk the same language in terms of physical and financial flows and also in terms of stocks and therefore their analytical capabilities can be usefully interconnected. The full chain margin enables to animate this interconnection.

## Key questions to address

1. Have you tested the competences of your supply chain management team in finance?
2. Have you developed specific training for non-supply chain managers on finance?
3. Have you integrated financial people in the supply chain management team?
4. Have you included financial parameters in your supply chain models?
5. Have you developed financial trade-offs?
6. How have you defined the holding rate to evaluate the cost of inventories?
7. How have you defined the WACC for assessing your investments in the supply chain fields?
8. Have you developed what-if scenarios testing the robustness of your supply chain model in case of peak oil and inflation rate growth and their impact on the end-to-end supply chain cost and the inventories cost?
9. What is the financialisation level of your supply chain management?
10. Have you implemented a full chain margin approach?

## PART B
# Design and animate the right supply chain models to create a competitive advantage

# Part B Introduction
# Fundamental analytics for agile and resilient supply chains

The purpose of this Part B introduction is to focus on two main analytical topics we consider business leaders have to be aware of in order to design agile and resilient supply chains.

## Topic #1: Demand pattern

As the mission of SCM is to fulfil the customers' demand, it is critical to analyse the demand pattern and its components. The following diagram shows explicitly the three main components of any demand:

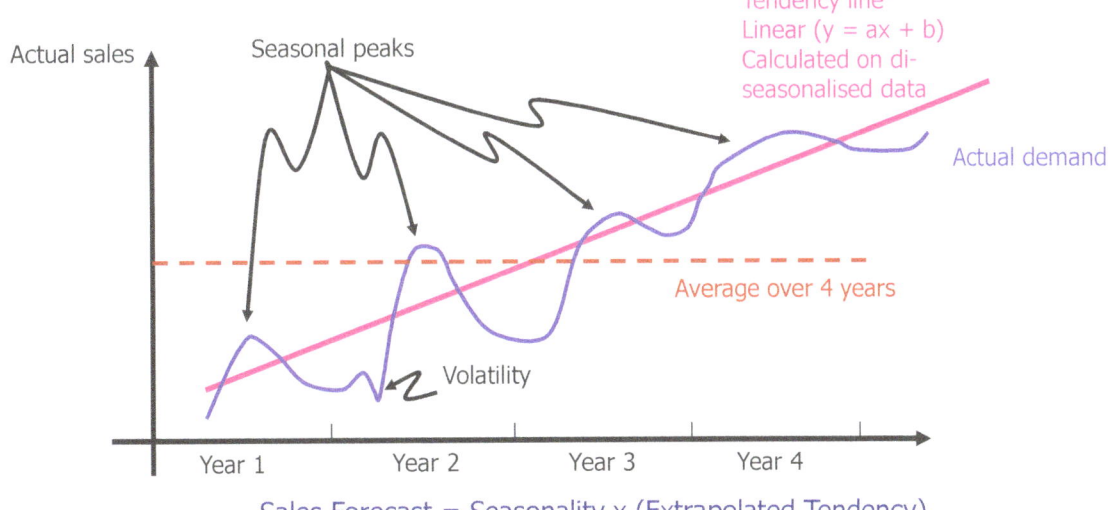

Demand pattern is based on trend, seasonality and volatility factor

Diag. 1: The components of the demand pattern

Those three components are:

- The **seasonality**, which is estimated over the last 3 years by calculating the monthly weight of the sales. Without seasonality the monthly index is 100/12 = 8.33 %. Here we talk about a monthly seasonal index, which is basically used for the S&OP process in order to dimension seasonal inventory or increasing the number of the production shifts (see Chapters 4, 5 and 13) but for highly seasonal businesses it can quite relevant and useful to calculate weekly seasonal index and even to identify the daily peak of the year, such as the day before Christmas or Valentine's Day in order to anticipate and to plan operational resources. As already shared in Chapter 5, the following graph displays the seasonal profile of the sell-out for a windshield replacement market in Poland:

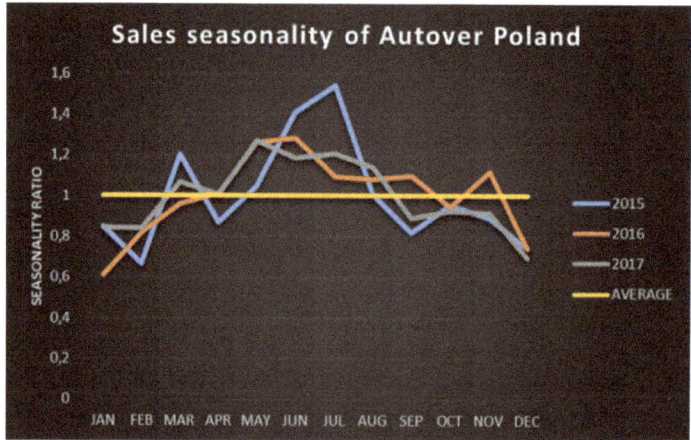

Diag. 2: Seasonal profile of the demand pattern (Autover, Poland, 2018)

There is a clear seasonality over 3 years even if the seasonal index varies year over year.

- The **trend**, which is estimated through a linear regression over 3 years considering de-seasonalised data, and enables us to point out a ramp up, a ramp down or no trend. This component is quite useful for the S&OP and CAPEX decisions (see Chapters 5 and 13).
- The **volatility**, which is the third component of the demand pattern. It measures the deviation of the daily sell-out around the mean. The mathematical parameter representing the volatility is the standard deviation. This is a fundamental component in order to avoid any shortage and especially by building up safety stock (see Chapter 13). The two following graphs enable us to visualise this notion of volatility and the link to the safety stock:

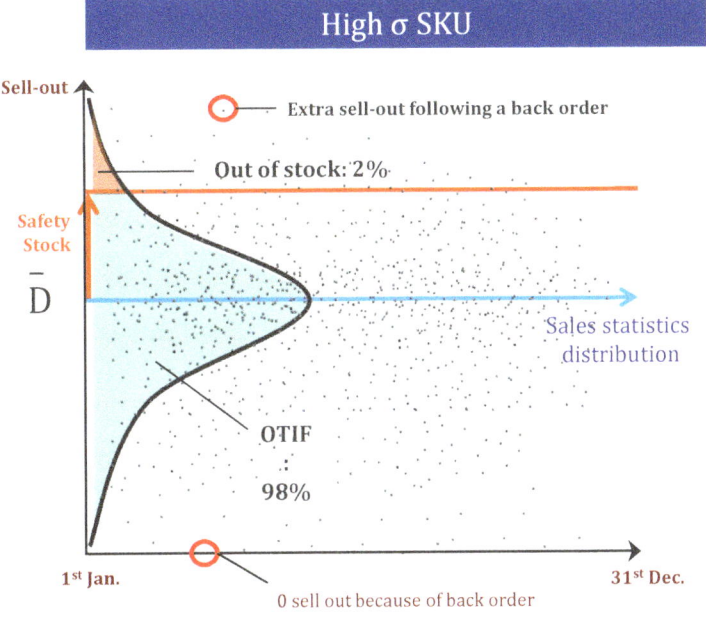

Diag. 3: Demand volatility and safety stock for high volatile product

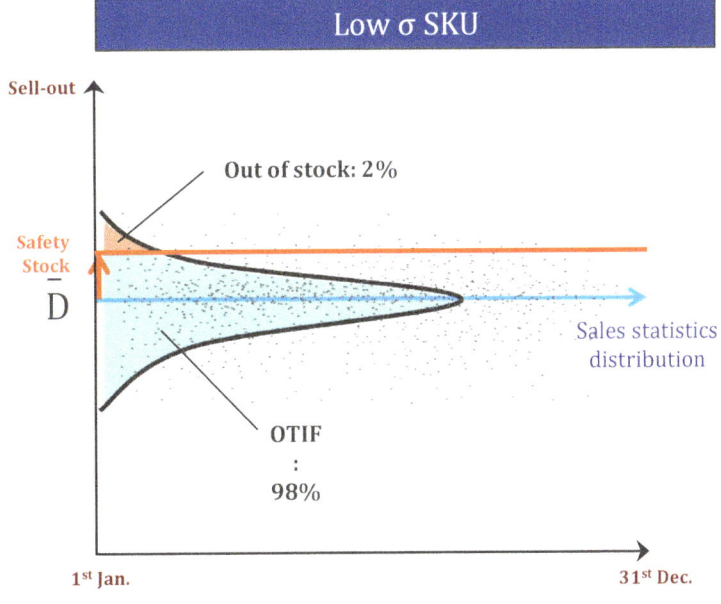

Diag. 4: Demand volatility and safety stock for low volatile product

- On the left graph, this is a demand pattern of high volatile SKU. Each point represents a daily sell-out. Before calculating the two statistical parameters, e.g. the mean $\bar{D}$ and the standard deviation $\sigma$, data has to be cleaned and pathologic points have to be pulled away. For instance, a day without sales could be the result of a back-order. In that case the actual demand was not zero and the point has to be pulled away. A few days after, the sell-out reached a very high level and that could be the result of an extra delivery including the previous back-order. This point is therefore pathologic and has to be pulled away. In this example, there is neither trend nor seasonality (the demand is flat) in order to just focus on the volatility factor. As you can see, the cloud of points is widespread and volatility is high. The horizontal blue line represents the statistical distribution of the sell-out and the curve shape looks like a bell curve, e.g. Gauss curve showing there is a 50% chance to sell less than the mean and a 50% chance to sell more than the mean. This curve shows the occurrence frequency of the sales volume. As volatility is high, this Gauss curve is pretty flat. If you want to avoid shortage and meet the demand, a possibility is to start every day with an extra volume above the mean and this extra quantity is called a safety stock. This is represented by a red arrow. As a positive consequence you will be able to serve the demand up to this level. On the graph, we have positioned this safety stock to be able to cover 98% of the cloud. This percentage is the OTIF (see Chapters 1 and 2). This example shows that the safety stock dimensioning is a trade-off decision (see Chapter 7). If you increase it:
  - The good news is OTIF will be higher and customer more satisfied
  - The bad news is the company will have consumed more cash

Therefore, this decision is neither a financial, nor a sales/marketing, nor a supply chain management decision but a general management decision based on a clear arbitration rule.

- The right graph displays a SKU, which has the same demand mean as the previous one but with a much lower standard deviation. The cloud of points is much more concentrated around the mean. Therefore, the Gauss curve representing the frequency of occurrence is much sharper and for the same OTIF target of 98%, the safety stock will be much lower. The risk shortage is much lower with a low $\sigma$ SKU.

Being able to model the demand pattern is key and leads to many decisions in terms of supply chain management at the strategic, tactical and operational levels.

## Topic #2: Segmenting and aggregating product: the ABC/XYZ/123 matrix

Facing a large product portfolio in terms of number of SKUs motivates you to segment it in order to identify a certain number of categories, each of them having a homogeneous 'behaviour' leading to design a specific supply chain management model to a given category. In other words, the idea is to simplify the product management from a SCM perspective by segmenting and grouping the SKUs into categories.

Therefore, the key question is to choose the right segmentation criteria. The first one is naturally linked to the sales volume for finished goods or consumption volume for raw materials and components. We apply the Pareto analysis and segment SKUs into the three ABC categories: A (fast movers or fast runners), 20% of the SKUs representing 80% of the volume; B, 30% of the SKUs representing 15% of the volume; and finally the category C (slow movers), representing 50% of the total number of SKUs and only 5% of the total volume.

In order to be more specific in the analysis and in the design of supply chain solutions, a second segmentation axis is quite useful. This second axis was identified through a project we ran for a B2B retailer in 2005. This retailer offered 1 million SKUs in its 2,000 branches. We decided to use the frequency of sales, which means how many times a year a given SKU is sold. In other words, this criterion measures the number of order lines over a full year for a given SKU. We applied the same Pareto analysis and segmented SKUs into the three ABC categories: X (daily products, which means products we sell every day): 20% of the SKUs representing 80% of the volume, Y (weekly or monthly products): 30% of the SKUs representing 15% of the volume and finally the category Z (yearly products sold a few times a year) representing 50% of the total number of SKUs and only 5% of the total order lines. This second criterion is a good estimation of the product volatility.

By matching those two segmentation criteria, we obtain the following matrix called ABC/XYZ matrix:

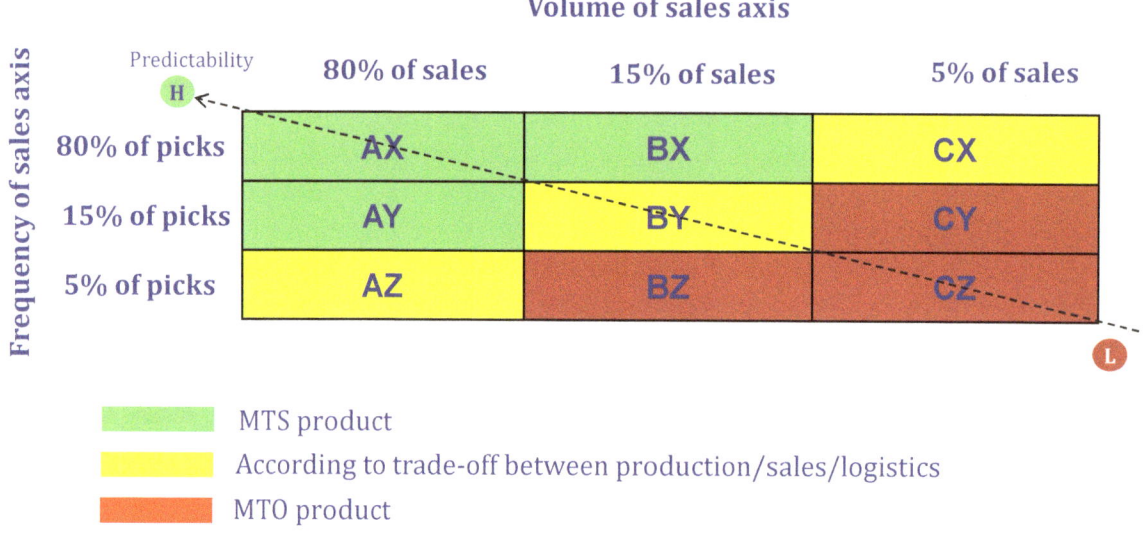

Diag. 5: ABC/XYZ matrix

On that matrix, ABC categories are in column and XYZ in lines, and generate nine categories described by a double letter. For instance:

- Products AX are sold in large volumes and almost every day.
- Products AZ are sold in large volumes but only once or twice a year. This is typical of products involved in large projects managed through ETO (Engineer-to-Order) (see Part A introduction) and generally managed through tenders.
- Products CX are sold almost every day but in small volumes.
- Finally, products CZ are sold in a very small volume and very few times over a year. We can really call those products 'nightmare', products at least from a SCM perspective!

The drawn diagonal dot line supports the fundamental rationale of this matrix; it shows that CZ products are highly unpredictable whereas AX products are highly predictable.

A decision could consist of deciding to phase out the CZ due to their unpredictability. This is a natural decision but it could be dangerous to do so for the two following reasons:

- Some CZ products, such as accessories, are sold with AX products within systems or solutions to customers.
- Some CZ products can generate a lot of margin. This is not rare that those CZ products generate 40% of the total gross margin of the company. Actually AX products are cash cow products and CZ can be star.

Therefore, this ABC/XYZ can benefit from being completed by gross margin as a complementary segmentation criterion such as displayed in the following table:

|  |  | A |  | B |  | C |  | TOTAL |  |
|---|---|---|---|---|---|---|---|---|---|
| X3 | #SKU | 7 | 28,0% | 2 | 8,0% | 0 | 0,0% | 9 | 36,0% |
|  | Sales | 100 735 258 | 66,9% | 12 021 435 | 8,0% | - | 0,0% | 112 756 693 | 74,9% |
|  | Stock | 1 360 758 | 61,1% | 105 485 | 4,7% | - | 0,0% | 1 466 243 | 65,8% |
| Y3 | #SKU | 2 | 8,0% | 5 | 20,0% | 1 | 4,0% | 8 | 32,0% |
|  | Sales | 16 598 161 | 11,0% | 12 020 607 | 8,0% | 961 976 | 0,6% | 29 580 744 | 19,6% |
|  | Stock | 170 712 | 7,7% | 267 224 | 12,0% | 37 244 | 1,7% | 475 180 | 21,3% |
| Z3 | #SKU | 0 | 0,0% | 1 | 4,0% | 7 | 28,0% | 8 | 32,0% |
|  | Sales | - | 0,0% | 1 589 848 | 1,1% | 6 678 270 | 4,4% | 8 268 118 | 5,5% |
|  | Stock | - | 0,0% | 51 129 | 2,3% | 234 105 | 10,5% | 285 234 | 12,8% |
| TOTAL | #SKU | 9 | 36,0% | 8 | 32,0% | 8 | 32,0% | 25 |  |
|  | Sales | 117 333 419 | 77,9% | 25 631 891 | 17,0% | 7 640 245 | 5,1% | 150 605 555 |  |
|  | Stock | 1 531 470 | 68,8% | 423 838 | 19,0% | 271 349 | 12,2% | 2 226 657 |  |

Diag. 6: ABC/XYZ /123 matrix

It is, of course, impossible to draw a 3D matrix, and in the previous table it is the ABC/XYZ/3 products that are displayed. By convention, which has to be customised according to the industry profile, products 1 have a higher gross margin than 40%, products 2 between 20% and 40% and products 3 less than 20%. In that example, the number of SKUs, the % of the sales value and the % of the stock level characterise each of the nine categories. We see that CZ3 products represent seven SKUs, e.g. 28% but only 4.4 % of the sales value and 10.5% of the stock value. For sure, those seven SKUs are candidates for being phased out to simplify the product portfolio.

## Take-away for leaders

The supply chain model and the supply chain management system highly depend on the understanding of the demand pattern. As a major take-away of the Covid-19 crisis, we believe that the demand has to be closer connected to the supply. The most appropriate supply chain solutions providing more agility and resilience should be based on a smart understanding of the demand.

This understanding will enable leaders to model, to simulate and to plan solutions at the strategic, tactical and operational levels.

The ABC/XYZ/123 matrix is a great tool for animating debates and leading to key decisions at the general management team level. Its construction enables us to decide a segmented approach related to:

- The supply chain planning strategies: MTS, MTO, late differentiation.
- The level of OTIF: higher for AX and lower for CZ, and more generally the level of service including the order-to-delivery lead-time.
- The stock level dimensioning for both safety and cycle stocks (see Chapter 13).
- The optimised layout of the warehouse.
- The phase in/phase out process.
- The follow up of the product life cycle from the introduction of a new product.

This matrix also prepares a supply chain management approach based on margin and is the entry point to the design of segmented supply chain management models (see Chapter 12).

## Key questions to address

1. Do you face a seasonal demand or a seasonal supply?
2. Have you assessed the volatility level of your demand at the product level or the distribution channel level or both?
3. Have you formalised what-if scenarios according to volatility assumptions?
4. Have you developed an ABC/XYZ/123 matrix to prepare key decisions at the management team level?
5. Have you identified the relevant segmentation criteria to segment the service offer, the supply chain strategy and the stock dimensioning?
6. How do you follow a given SKU over its product life cycle?
7. Have you a robust phase in–phase out process?

# Chapter 9
# Innovate and invest in the right digital supply chain operating system

## Key ideas

The supply chain operating system describes which solutions have to be implemented to manage a given supply chain. This operating system has to be designed according to the value equation of the supply chain model generated from the five-parameter value equation (see Chapter 1). The value equation formalises the priorities in terms of business value creation by supply chain management. The fundamental idea is that the choice of the operating solutions should depend on the objectives of value equation (see Chapter 10).

As displayed in the diagram 1, the supply chain operating system is structured around five building blocks. We differentiate:

- Two structural building blocks: governance/KPIs and processes
- Three resource-based building blocks: people, operations and IT/data

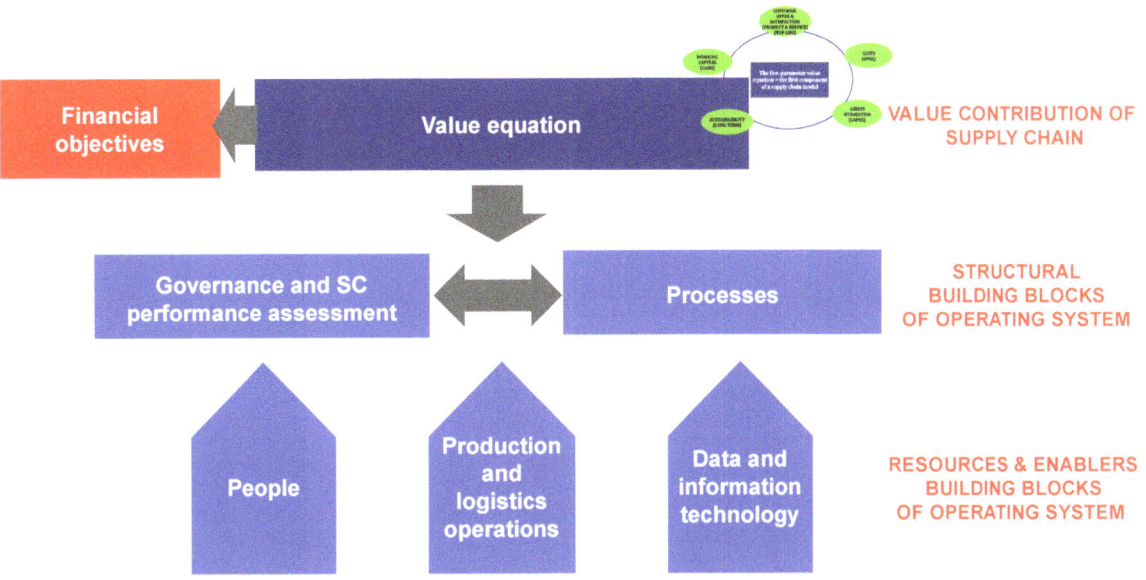

Diag. 1: The five building blocks of the supply chain operating system

## 1. The two structural building blocks

### a) Governance and KPIs

The two key points related to governance are to:

- Define allocation of accountabilities related to missions, which are generally supported by processes.
- Formalise the rules of arbitration especially used in the S&OP (see Chapter 13). Those rules translate the priorities from the 5-parameter value equation.

We generally use the RACI methodology (R: Responsible, A: Accountable, C: Consulted, I: Informed) to define the accountabilities. We propose to take the example of the demand forecast process. The governance question is: who is accountable for the forecast accuracy? In the following diagram, we study two different governance models:

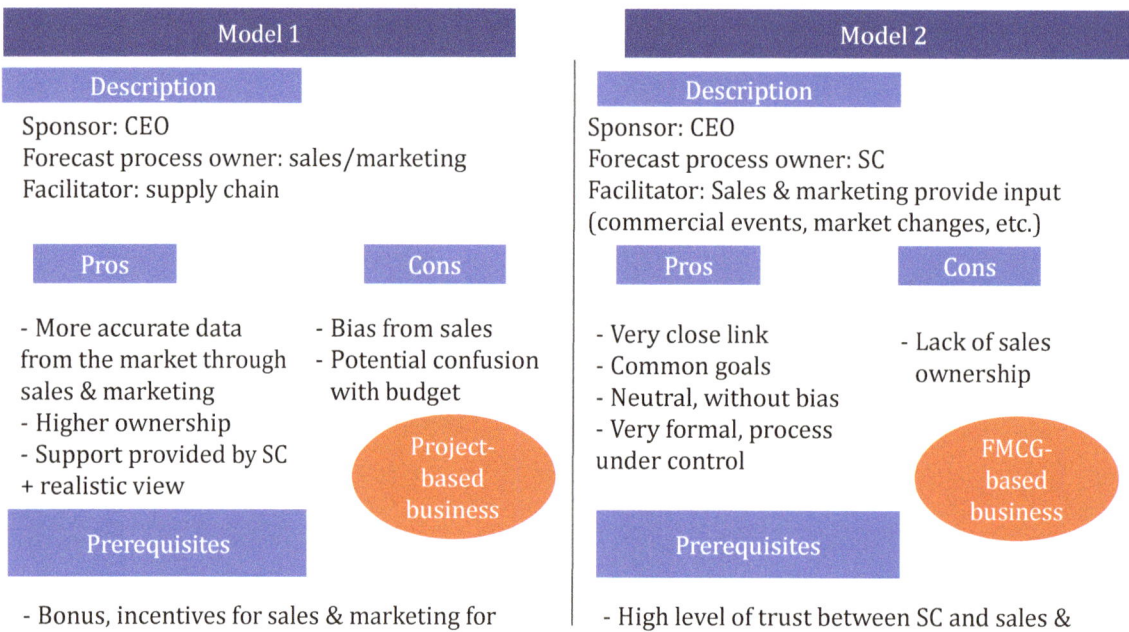

Diag. 2: Comparison of two governance models for demand forecast

In both models the CEO is the sponsor. In model 1, sales/marketing is accountable for the forecast accuracy, and supply chain plays the role of facilitator by analysing and modelling the demand pattern, cleaning and crunching data and proposing forecast. In model 2, the accountability roles are the opposite and the sales/marketing role just exists to provide information on commercial events, introduction of new products and market changes. Each governance model has pros, cons and prerequisites to be successful and fits actually better according to the business context: model 1 works well for project-based industry with tenders and probability of success, whereas model 2 is quite appropriate to FMCG (fast moving consumer goods) with recurrent sales volume based on statistical predictive models. Here again the supply chain model has to be segmented and it shows that governance has to be closely defined with the processes.

In this first structural building block KPIs have to defined (see Chapter 11).

## b) Processes

There are five major processes (see Chapter 13) to design within the operating system of a given supply chain model:

- The demand forecast.
- The S&OP/IBP.
- The supply chain planning strategies: MTS, MTO and the decoupling point.
- The inventories dimensioning.
- The phase in (introduction of a new product) and the phase out (end-of-life of products).

## 2. The three resource-based building blocks

## a) People

A supply chain relies fundamentally on people. We have to consider two main categories of people:

- The non-professionals of supply chain. As mentioned in the introduction of Part A, everyone is part of supply chain and impacts by his or her decision directly or indirectly the performance of that supply chain. Therefore, this is key to educate them according to the governance model and to the performance drivers they control. Dedicated trainings have to be designed and delivered to those people.
- The professionals of supply chain. The growth of degrees developed by both business and engineering schools at the level of Specialised Masters (Sciences and Business Administration) and PhDs is amazing and the portfolio of programs worldwide is quite large. Here, this is essential that those people have to be trained on the specific field of SCM, but complementary fields have to be addressed, especially business strategy, marketing and finance. Complementary to those hard skills, the professionals of supply chain have to develop their management and leadership skills especially on the following axes:
  - Collaborative mindset
  - Listener
  - Discipline supportive
  - Customer-centric
  - Creative

- Neutrality
- Ability to build up discussion between different functions
- Communicator
- Builder of trust
- Resilience

Those leadership skills are key as supply chain managers have absolutely no hierarchical authority on the players impacting the supply chain performance. Therefore, their influencing leadership is the right way to get the overall supply chain performance, and supply chain managers, thanks to their cross-functional lens, are great potential business leaders.

The World Economic Forum has identified in the job landscape for 2022 new jobs in development and growth such as data analysts and scientists, AI and machine-learning specialists, big and smart data specialists and 4.0 technology specialists. Those jobs are highly connected to supply chain management.

## b) Operations

This building block covers both logistics and industrial operations. The four generic production models are job shop, batch flow, assembly line and continuous flow. The decision to apply one of those models depends on the market positioning, mostly characterised by the price, the volume and the level of customisation. The two extreme poles are commodity vs premium as displayed with the following diagram:

**Strategic market positioning**

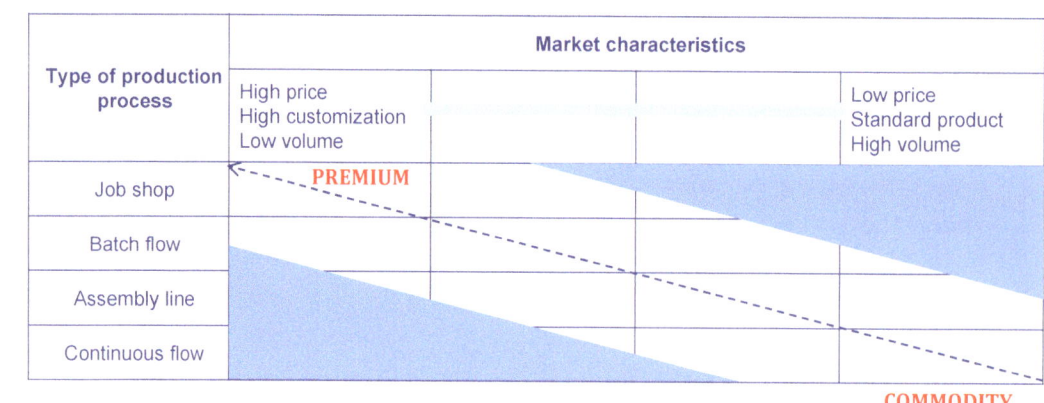

Diag. 3: Consistency of the factory model with the strategic market positioning

Production operations are not under the authority of SCM, but the way production is organised generates a lot of interest for SCM due to the following topics, which are linked to SC planning:

- The type of production process has an impact on the supply chain lead-time. In a job shop environment (satellite, luxury car, military aircraft), the production lead-time is measured in a number of months, whereas in a continuous flow the production lead-time can be in a couple of hours. This parameter has an impact on (see introduction Part A):
  - The overall end-to-end supply chain lead-time.
  - The positioning of the decoupling point.
  - The required horizon of planning.
- The level of work-in-progress (WIP) and finished goods stocks, generally higher in batch flow compared to continuous flow as a consequence of the level of integration.
- The ratio between manual vs automated operations, which impacts the end-to-end supply chain cost.

The logistics operations are a key parameter of the SC operating system. The main topics that are addressed by logistics are the following:

- Warehousing operations: receiving goods, storing, handling, picking, packing, shipping.
- Cross-docking operations through platforms.
- Transportation.
- Order-to delivery tracking.
- Choice of incoterms.
- Customs operations.
- Subcontracted operations to 3PL (third Party Logistics).

There are a lot of innovations in smart logistics and Amazon has developed a lot of patents in logistics technologies such as drones, a new generation of logistics building, speech recognition, image analysis, urban logistics, robots and automated storage and picking systems.

## c) Data and IT

In order to facilitate the understanding of those enabling building blocks, we have differentiated the physical operations from the digital solutions. But actually this an artificial distinction and 4.0 supply chain solutions and digital supply chain solutions embed operations, data and IT. This is what we call the digital continuity (see diagram 4), which means:

- Developing the horizontal (end-to-end from suppliers to customers) and vertical, from the shop floor where operations are executed such as MES (manufacturing execution system) to the decision-making tool such as APS (advanced planning solutions) **connectivity.**
- Getting the value from the collected **data** by analysing them, using them in models to support decisions or in predictive tools.
- Using **smart automation** tools such as robots, AM (additive manufacturing) like 3D printing or AR (augmented reality such as Google lens).

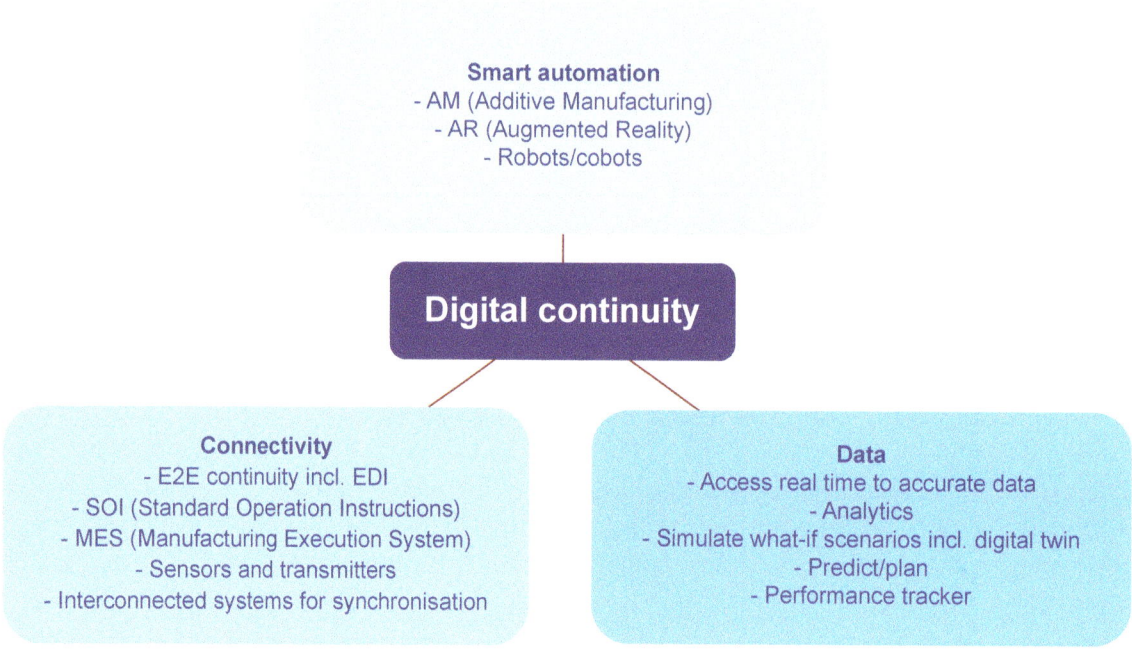

Diag. 4: Digital continuity

Those digital solutions potentially provide the following benefits:

- Leverage end-to-end visibility and especially on the sell-out (Who? Where? What? How much?), and then on the procurement and the production resources.
- Acceleration of flows based on IT and data integration for a real time and integrated actionable decision.
- Prediction, if predictability is possible (maintenance, events, sales volumes, supply, missing parts), and if not decision-making based on real time data and analytics.
- Capability of scenario simulation with financial impacts (product, price, margin, load allocation, route-to-market, new businesses, etc.).
- Synchronised planning processes based on massive collaboration at the interfaces without underestimating the need for trust between the stakeholders of the end-to-end supply chain.
- Faster supply chain planning processes to react to business events.
- Ergonomics for workforce and productivity based on standards.
- Data accuracy (master data management) coupled with smart data supporting autonomous decisions.

Those digital solutions require at least for their successful implementation two prerequisites:

- A high level of collaboration between players in order to break down the organisational silos.
- The implementation of an ERP to support a seamless and collaborative organisation.

Part B  Design and animate the right supply chain models to create a competitive advantage

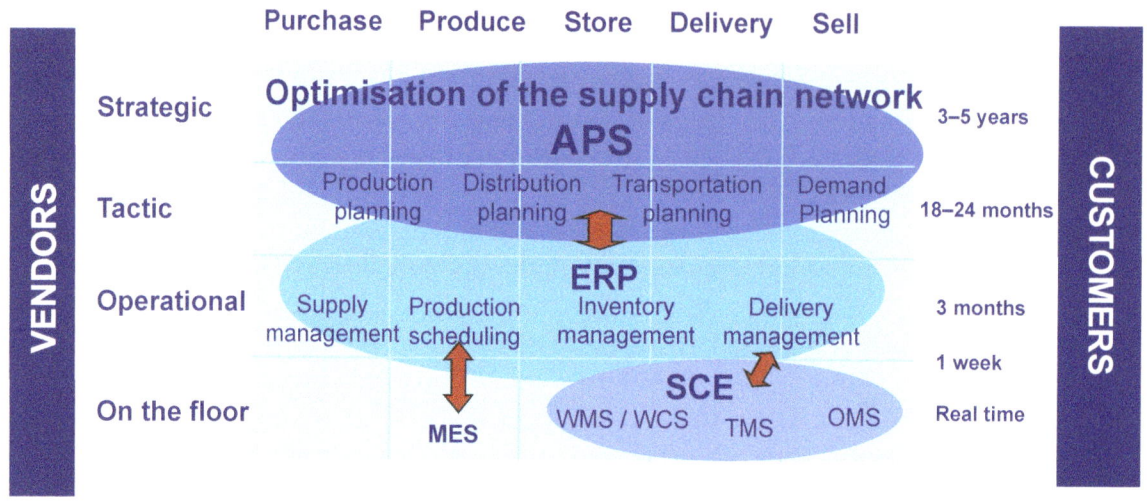

Diag. 5: The IT solutions in supply chain management

# Testimony from Aera Technology

Ram KRISHNAN, Chief Marketing Officer, Aera Technology.

Gonzalo BENEDIT, General Manager EMEA, Aera Technology.

Loïs GUILLEMAILLE, Client Partner, Aera Technology.

*What is your analysis of the current and future challenges related to supply chain?*

Supply chains are talking about E2E visibility in 2020, which is the current topic given Covid. If you look at the other side, we live in an era of post business intelligence/control tower world. That clearly proves that either:

(1) Supply chains have mis-adopted business intelligence/control tower solutions,

(2) Technology and consulting vendors didn't deliver on the promise, or

(3) There is systemic failure to look deeply at facts presented by data on hand and lead organisational decision-making with data. Digitalisation still being a lip-service is the problem.

We see the critical challenge to be #3, which is cultural, organisational, and systemic. We anticipate the future of supply chains to be AGILE, SUSTAINABLE, and RESPONSIBLE. Supply chains of the future would be able to plan, adapt, and act effectively and efficiently to reach their stated goals.

*Founders of Aera Technology have a long business background in technologies applied to supply chain. Can we say we face a change of paradigm in terms of IT solutions applied to supply chain?*

Absolutely. With the availability of incredible computing power, storage, and bandwidth, we truly have an opportunity to transform supply chains to digital supply networks fundamentally. Aera is leveraging this to deliver that transformation, connecting and harmonizing all internal and external supply chain data in real-time, continuously thinking and learning, and autonomously taking actions. We summarise it by saying it moves from an era of people doing the work supported by machines to an era of machines doing the work guided by people.

*What is exactly behind the terminology « Cognitive Automation »?*

Cognitive Automation is the automation and augmentation of decision-making and execution across enterprise-wide business processes. Please note that it's not just about automating and augmenting work; it's about evolving the enterprise and up-levelling the nature of work for people. Cognitive automation looks at how decisions are being made and improve performance and outcomes. It opens up new possibilities and opportunities and enables digital non-natives to operate like digital natives (think how it would be for a 100-year-old company to run and compete like Amazon). It creates long-run economies of scale and societal value.

*Can you explain the role of AI in Aera Technology solutions?*

There are two broad approaches to AI. (1) AI as an add-on (2) AI as embedded.

Aera embeds AI and orchestrates intelligence in core decision-making processes in supply chains. For example, forecasting, predicting the risk of stock out, or risk of delays in deliveries. Aera leverages an elastic AI layer that provides the right intelligence in context. It also releases data scientists and engineers from volumes of manual work involved in operationalising data science models into specific business processes.

*Based on your experience with your customers, what are the key success factors for getting a successful Aera Technology solution implementation?*

Fantastic question. Experiment and scale-out. Find the top two use cases and build a roadmap to deploy those while building new ones, leveraging a single platform for strategic and tactical decision-making across the supply chain. When scaling, do not forget change management is crucial for success. Aera delivers the fastest time to value with this approach.

*In which business context such solution will be providing the highest benefit to the business?*

Cognitive automation allows us to drive efficiency and agility in decision-making to optimise operations across cash cost and service level while minimizing waste and environmental impact. The highest benefit comes from taking actions on the long tail of small events happening across the supply chain, which humans cannot detect in a timely manner and assess cost benefits and feasibility of all alternative options to make a decision. At the same time, a machine can continuously course-correct. Starting points will vary depending on the challenges faced by the business.

Ideally, most significant and immediate benefits come from reimagining your forecasting/demand planning, strategic and tactical inventory placements, trade promotion management, order fulfilment, and logistics execution processes, etc. The strategic benefit comes from interdisciplinary processes – e.g., supply chain finance, reimagining S&OP, and Integrated Business Planning (IBP), etc.

**This book talks to cross-industry business leaders. AI is quite new for everyone. What are your final words to convince such leaders at least to test such innovative solutions?**

Don't hesitate, take the leap, design experiments to scale, and beware of pilot purgatory. Your peers and big organizations are already doing it right NOW. First movers will get a competitive advantage by starting cognitive automation early and harvesting decision history to improve their performance continuously. In the digital businesses, the entry barriers are now more in the data collected than in the technology, and it will soon be the case in the supply chain. The future is already here. Are you ready to embrace it?

## Take-away for leaders

The digitalisation of the supply chains is a must but more than ever such investments have to be selective and done accordingly to the five-parameter value equation. Benefits related to digitalisation are potentially numerous but they have to be clearly formalised.

As the most cross-functional activity, SCM requires a clear and formal governance model. Accountabilities have to be defined for all key processes. Sales forecast accuracy, stocks level and production asset return are at stake through the governance. SCM is a matter of monitoring the business not only by matching demand and supply but also by facilitating the decision-making process. As we see in Chapter 13 with the S&OP, those processes rely on people, governance, formal steps, data and IT, which are all of them building blocks of the SC operating system.

We advise not to underestimate the role of people for generating the SC performance. Investing in the right people with the appropriate technical and management skills is key. Digital solutions provide fast automated people-free operations, but designing the models, providing the right parameters, challenging the data beyond the machine learning and making the final decision for outstanding situations after escalation relies on humans.

## Key questions to address

1. Have you formalised the building blocks of the SC operating model?
2. Have you assessed their strengths and their weaknesses?
3. Have you a clear governance model consistently with the main SC processes?
4. Have you developed specific trainings in SCM for the business managers?
5. Do you impose professional certifications to your supply chain managers?
6. Do you manage the mobility of people from business management positions to supply chain management and vice-versa?
7. Do you consider logistics as part of your core business or not?
8. What is the level of digitalisation of your SC?
9. Do you have a clear vision of the benefits of the SC digitalisation for your business?
10. If your SC is still poorly digitalised do you have a clear idea of the digitalisation roadmap?

# Chapter 10

# Create a competitive advantage based on the second paradigm of SCM: the fair value

## Key ideas

### 1. The supply chain model

We define a supply chain model through its two components:

- The value equation based on the selected and prioritised parameters (see Chapter 1).
- The operating system based on its five building blocks (see Chapter 9).

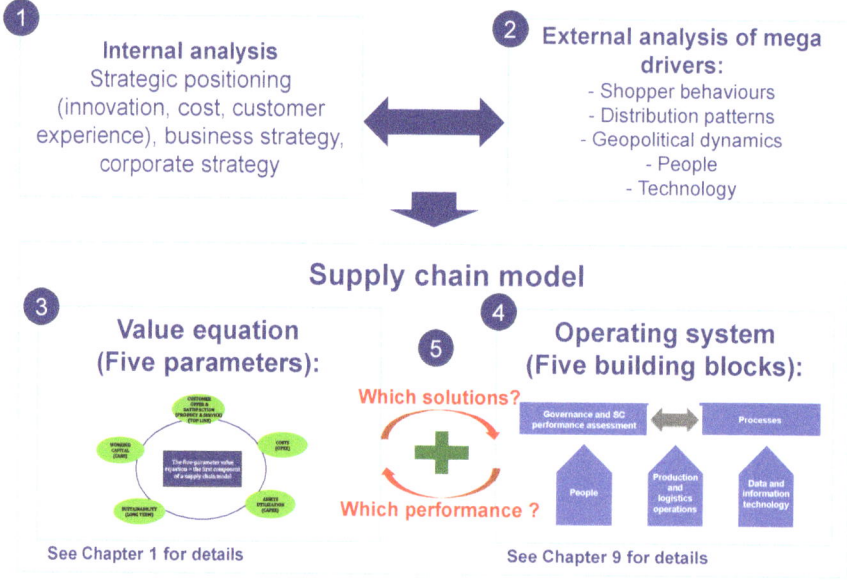

Diag. 1: Supply chain model

In order to design it, we recommend making two complementary analyses, which have both a strategic dimension:

- The **internal analysis**, which enables to define:
  - The **strategic positioning** of the company. Theory and practice show that there are only three ways to get a market leadership and you have to make a choice as shown in the following diagram:

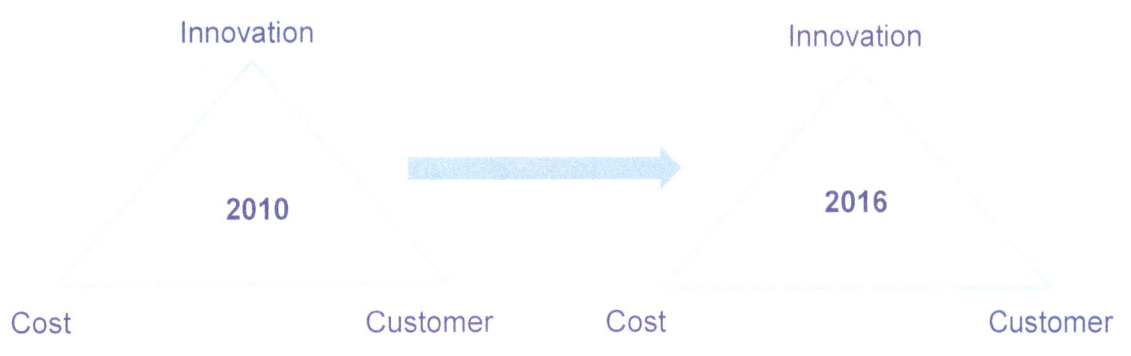

Diag. 2: Strategic positioning

In this above example, in 2010, the strategic positioning was innovation. As this company was facing increasing problems to create a competitive advantage through innovation, the top managers decided not to choose a cost-based leadership in order to avoid low margin and to commoditise their business, but to strategically focus on customer intimacy and experience to get a competitive advantage.

- The **business strategy** of the company, which consists of determining the key success factors for a given business in order to improve its positioning on the markets and to build up a sustainable competitive advantage. A take-away of that analysis is to build up a business model based on a value proposition and value architecture. The value equation of the SC model and the value proposition of the business model have to be consistent and the operating system with the value architecture. Then, the link between the business strategy and the SC model is obvious.
- The **corporate strategy** of the company is focused on the strategic management of its activities and business portfolio. Here the link between the corporate strategy

and the SC model relies on the opportunity to differentiate the SC models according to the business (see Chapter 12).

- Five mega-drivers potentially impacting the SC model design have to be considered in the **external analysis,** as listed in this table:

| Mega-drivers | Main characteristics of evolution |
|---|---|
| Shoppers behaviours | Responsible and local shopping <br> Higher customisation <br> Simplicity and wellness <br> 24/7 possibility <br> Valuable customer experience |
| Distribution channels | Omnichannel <br> Growth of online <br> Concentration of purchasing groups for big retailers <br> Convergence of B2B and B2C <br> Development of peer-to-peer (P2P) <br> Reinforcement of the private labels |
| Geopolitics and | Shift from BRIC (Brazil, Russia, India, China) to MINT infrastructures (Malaysia, Indonesia, Nigeria, Thailand) <br> Climate change <br> Dual polarity: global and local <br> New infrastructures connecting regions (bridges, railway) and facilitating flows (free zone logistics) |
| People | Gen Y and Z <br> Mobile work <br> Home office outside from big cities <br> People assessment based on attitudes versus competences |
| Technologies | 4.0 and digital solutions |

It is clear that those drivers participate in the VUCA (Volatile, Uncertain, Complex, Ambiguous) world.

Both value equation and operating system should derive from those internal and external analyses.

## 2. Create a competitive advantage through the fair value

In the strategic analysis, the creation of a competitive advantage is based on the gap between the Willingness to Pay (WTP) and the cost. This gap is composed of the customer value or benefit and the firm profit (see diag. 3). You get a competitive advantage if this gap is higher than the competitor's. The WTP is a fundamental notion, which is the result of the market itself in three dimensions:

- The nature of the business.
- The satisfaction level of the customers related to your offer, which can be measured by the NPS, (see Chapters 1 and 2).
- The competitors' performance.

The WTP is highly correlated to the value perception of the customers. SCM plays a key role in executing the promise of the offer to the customers (see Chapters 1 and 2).

As displayed in the following graph, the gap between WTP and the full cost covers both the company profit and the customer value, which is the customer benefit beyond the price. This price is the result of a trade-off between the company looking for a higher profit and the customer looking to maximise their benefit.

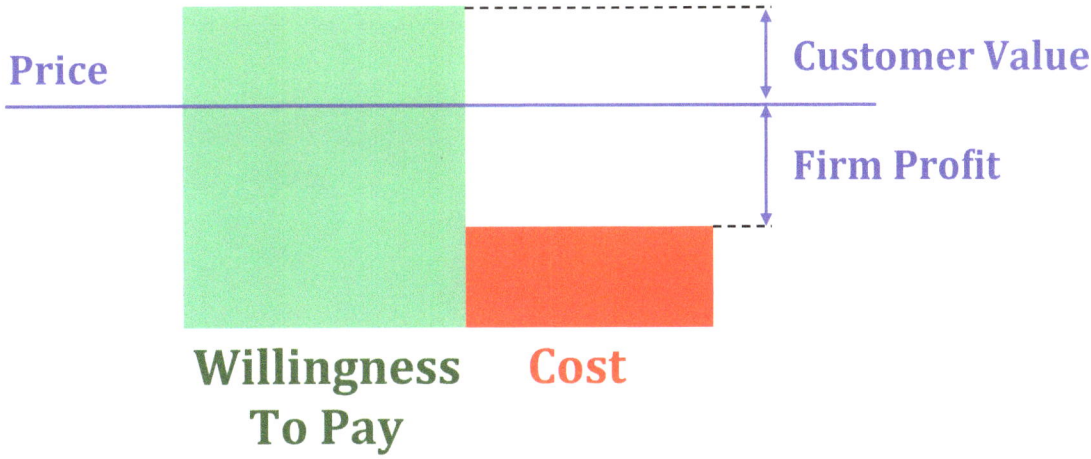

Diag. 3: Willingness to Pay, cost and price (Lehman-Ortega and al. 2019)

We have applied this theory to SCM through the model presented in diagram 2. The vertical axis positions the WTP and the horizontal axis represents the level of SC complexity. This level of complexity can be easily assessed for a given company in a given business through three major axes: products (SKUs, new products, etc.), customers (customers, diversity, geographic location) and supply (plants, vendors, geographic location). Those three axes can be completed by factors such as: the revenue growth, the number of interfaces in the company and the demand volatility. It is important to differentiate the complexity factors, which are under your control, and external factors, such as the demand volatility, which you do not control.

The model predicts that the SC complexity, in other words the end-to-end SC cost, has to be consistent with the WTP. This is the meaning of the grey diagonal on the graph. If the SC complexity is much higher than the WTP, the company destroys value and will disappear. The target consists of being above the diagonal by having a WTP much higher than the end-to-end SC cost. We call this second paradigm of SCM the **fair value** in order to keep in mind that:

- The SC operating system has to be aligned with the WTP.
- An over offer such as an over service generates a fake value and destroys value.

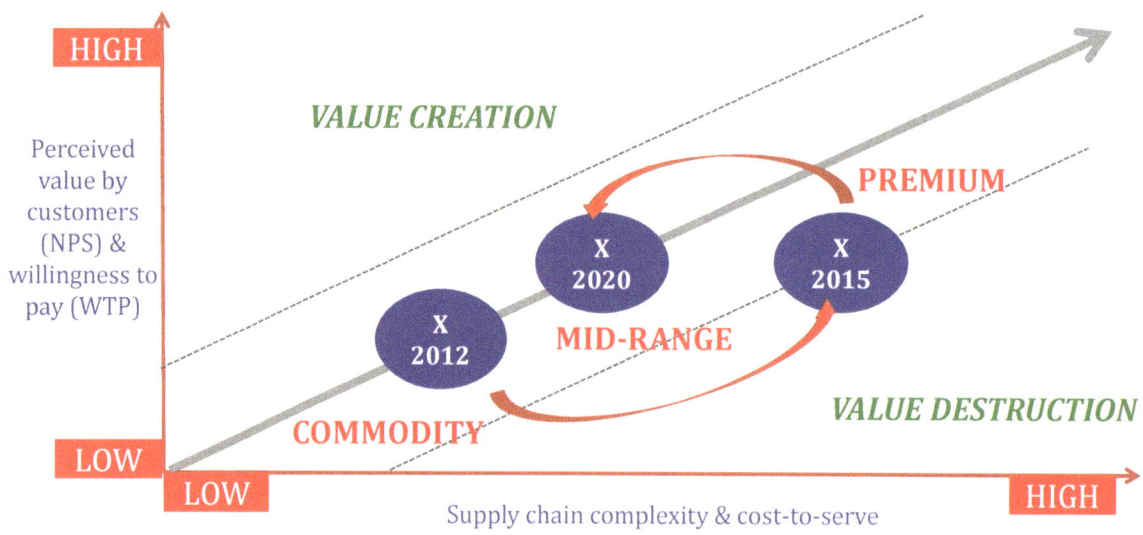

Diag. 4: The second paradigm of SCM: the Fair Value
(example from a manufacturing company in the construction industry)

We designed this model thanks to a company we worked for a few years ago. The blue bubbles provide the steps of the story:

- In 2012, the positioning of this company was consistent in terms of fair value.
- Due to a crisis in that industry, in order to stimulate the revenue generation the top management decided especially to increase the number of SKUs (x3) by applying a micro-marketing strategy and to close down some plants to play on the volume–price elasticity equation. As a result, the SC complexity increased, as well as the stock level, the logistics and the transportation costs, whereas all surveys showed that the NPS has not increased at the same pace. This is why in 2015 the fair value equation was destroyed.
- This is why we decided to design and to implement a SC transformation plan essentially to simplify the SC model in order to go back to the fair value diagonal in 2020.

A competitive advantage is generated if your own gap between the WTP and the SC cost is higher than the average gap of the industry you compete in. There are three ways to generate a competitive advantage:

- Increasing WTP for the same SC cost.
- Decreasing SC cost for the same WTP.
- Increasing WTP and decreasing SC cost in order to get a dual advantage.

SCM is definitely a key leverage to get such competitive advantage by:

- Developing a differentiation strategy based on offers of both products and services, as long as customers are ready to pay for such offers. It means as long as they perceive and value that differentiation. If the competitors have the same price, the customers will be attracted by the supplier that has the higher WTP, in order to maximise their perceived value.
- Segmenting the customer value, as customers' expectations are not the same (see Chapter 12).
- Eliminating non-value-added operations and streamlining the end-to-end SC in order to reduce the end-to-end SC cost.

# Testimony from OCP

Mme Nada El MAJDOUB, Executive VP Performance Management, OCP

Mr Marouane AMEZIANE, Executive VP Strategy and Corporate Development, OCP

*What are the business expectations from supply chain management?*

The supply chain of a company like OCP is complex by design. The complexity is threefold: product-related, spatial and temporal. Indeed, OCP product portfolio encompasses the entire value chain of phosphorus: phosphate rock, phosphoric acid and phosphate-based fertilisers. Each of these segments contains several products with different physical and chemical requirements. For example, the phosphoric acid purity depends on its use: fertiliser grade, feed grade for animal feeds and food-grade (the purest) for human food additives. In addition, the complexity of the supply chain is spatial: OCP operates in three major axes, with each axis comprising mining sites, which are landlocked, chemical site located on the coast and port infrastructure. Lastly, there is also a temporal complexity as some tactical decisions need to be made in advance and they directly impact the planning of operations. For example, the mining plan and the raw materials purchasing are set before the order book is fully finalised. Handling these intertwined levels of complexity is a challenge for OCP. The Group has developed and continues to enhance decision-helping tools for arbitrating between the use of scarce resources and making data-driven decisions under uncertainty. The stakes are high for the company as recent studies assess the value creation in debottlenecking the supply chain at a double-digit percentage of EBITDA.

Pockets of value exist along the entire supply chain, ranging from capacity increases to debottlenecking of industrial assets and port infrastructure to the ability to respond more quickly to short-term demand and the realisation of optimisations through an effective S&OP.

This complexity is set to increase even further as the Group embarks on the next S-curve, marked notably by higher product customisation, a closer proximity to the farmer and the exploration of adjacencies in by-products. This new S-curve relies on four strategic pillars: capacity leadership, cost leadership, industrial flexibility and commercial agility. The strategy affects all levels of the supply chain, which is a fundamental enabler for its execution.

Thus, a sound management of the supply chain is essential for:

- Executing strategy, and
- Capturing and unlocking value on (i) the long term through a supply chain design that allows for maximum flexibility and on (ii) short term through operational optimisations.

In addition, a good management of the supply chain allows the mitigation of a number of risks including shortage of raw materials, port constraints (loading and unloading challenges), non-availability of production assets because of bad maintenance scheduling leading to missed business opportunities.

**Supply Chain within OCP is embedded within the performance management. Can you explain the rationale of that organisation?**

Supply chain is transversal in nature. It involves many stakeholders from the industrial operations and industrial development, commercial (sales, raw materials procurement, freight) and finance (management/cost control and working capital).

Objectives of these stakeholders may be conflicting. The objective of the supply chain function is to align all stakeholders towards a common target as a global optimum (better than the sum of local optimums) in an effort to boost overall Group performance. This is why supply chain is embedded into the performance management department.

The following examples illustrate the transversal nature of the supply chain and the importance of pursuing a global optimum. Assume a salesperson finds a great opportunity for a high-grade rock with a premium of A$/t on the average-grade rock. In normal circumstances, that would be a great opportunity for OCP. If at the moment of the sale, the inventory level of high-grade rock is very low and the extraction cost of the rock is at B$/t (with B>A) versus C$/t in normal conditions (with C<A<B), due to some exceptional constraint, the sale should not be concluded, unless the premium is increased. A similar situation can occur on the chemical side: if a specific link of the

supply chain (sulfuric acid production for example) is under pressure, then the marginal cost of sulfuric acid is very high. The information is communicated to sales people to incentivise them to sell products that need less to none sulfuric acid. These two examples show the interest of transversal KPIs, as stakeholders may not have access to the same information at the same time.

The common target is the optimisation of the margin on variable costs. Both topline and costs lever are considered, hence a higher optimisation potential.

Performance management, as a neutral stakeholder, has a 360-degrees view of the end-to-end supply chain and can thus make recommendations factoring-in all potential impacts of actions and initiatives. For example, a cost-saving initiative in terms of raw materials specific consumption has a far broader impact than the mere raw materials cost saving. Indeed, the initiative frees up capacity, allowing for more volume loading, thus serving more clients and generating more value. The supply chain management team, within performance management, can quantify these gains, proposing holistic recommendations.

**The supply chain management team fosters collaboration between multiple stakeholders, who may face contradictory objectives. How are the different interactions handled within OCP? What are the main challenges faced?**

Through the setting of a common target consisting in the optimisation of the margin on variable costs, supply chain management fosters collaboration between multiple stakeholders and aligns objectives. As mentioned before, the global optimum is different from the sum of local optimums. A global optimum may call for reducing production level at a specific site due for example to shortage of raw materials whereas local optimum would push every unit head to saturate production.

The S&OP process is led by the business steering entity for different time horizons (yearly to monthly).

It starts with data collection from industrial, commercial and financial teams (capacity level), specific consumption, maintenance schedule, global sales portfolio by client (price and volume), strategic objectives (e.g. contractual volumes that need to be served), tactical moves, raw materials purchasing constraints, cost structure by product and by step of production ... This first step involves many iterations to challenge the assumptions.

The data is then ingested into the supply chain model that runs to optimise the margin on variable costs. Scenarios are built factoring-in risks in terms of production shortage, weather conditions, and commercial negotiation window and product prioritisation.

The output consists of concrete actions/recommendations for each scenario: production by line and product and volume allocation by client (optimal client portfolio) and a ranking of the underlying margins. If, for example, commercial wants to sell a product not well ranked to serve a particular client, then it will need to review its pricing for it to be more competitive in the optimal portfolio.

The model also computes the shadow prices or the marginal cost of the different products in the supply chain. Indeed, depending on the different bottlenecks and supply constraints (raw material prices, capacity limitation, etc.) the shadow price can vary significantly depending on different supply chain configurations.

A precise understanding of the shadow prices has two objectives. In the short term, the objective is to assess the profit and loss of arbitrage between products and clients. In the long term, it helps tailor investment to address the most critical bottlenecks, thus maximising value creation.

The recommendation is then submitted to the business steering committee (@executive level for quarterly and yearly exercises) to select the most probable scenario. This scenario becomes the sales and production targets for the next period.

Full cross-departmental transparency is achieved because all stakeholders have access to the model. They can run simulations and quantify the impact of their actions on the supply chain.

## *What are the main projects the supply chain team works on?*

The supply chain team has worked on several projects. The supply chain model is based on linear programming under constraints (industrial, logistics, commercial, etc.). It was first built in 2010. It evolved from a simple Excel tool to a digitalised platform powered by sophisticated language programming (Python).

The supply chain model was designed to work in pair with a market model. The market model aimed at forecast price and demand dynamics based on OCP and its competitor moves. Objective of the model is to help OCP commercial team allocate volumes between markets.

The team has worked in order to unify them into a model that combines both to assess how the supply chain dynamics interact with the market supply/demand tension in order to find a global equilibrium that maximises OCP margin.

This project was conducted through a tight collaboration with MIT Operational research department and has led to many strategic projects. For example, a model was developed to optimise the port loading at Jorf port, which represents a critical link in the OCP supply chain.

The further collaboration with MIT will include demand forecast, refining the Jorf loading model to extend its scope and use robust optimisation to assess and address the uncertainties inherent to the supply chain like production or ships delays.

The team is also applying for the Edelman Award.

***Do you consider supply chain management can be a leverage of the company transformation?***

Supply chain management is certainly a strong lever for the Group transformation. It promotes new ways of working, new governance and new standards. By championing the use of analytics and digital tools, it contributes to the spreading and adoption of new operating models and collaborative decision-making. The pursuit of a global optimum forces the multiple stakeholders to collaborate and factor-in impacts of their actions and moves beyond their perimeter, hence breaking the silos that may exist.

Furthermore, the high level of integration via digital tools and models offers transparency and improves overall decision-making through the establishment of one single data source of truth.

## Take-away for leaders

The starting point is to decide your strategic position in the market. Keep in mind, you have only three possibilities representing a triangle: innovation, cost or customer, and you have to be focused. If you want to die, the best solution is to be in the gravity centre of the triangle. A cost-driven strategy will lead to a very different supply chain model compared to a customer-driven strategy.

The SC operating system has to be aligned with the value equation, which has been prioritised according to the strategic position. To be aligned means applying the paradigm of fair value, meaning avoiding any over offer customers are not ready to pay for and designing and selecting SC solutions that provide the expected customer value, no more no less.

SCM enables us to get a competitive advantage by increasing the gap between the WTP and the cost-to-serve. This is the result of a differentiation strategy stimulating the WTP based on a clear positioning strategy and of the operational excellence of SC based on lean and simplification actions.

Complexity can be acceptable from a strategic perspective as long as it creates entry barriers to competitors and customers are ready to pay for the extra cost generated by that complexity. Each complexity factor has to be analysed and eliminated or valued to customers.

## Key questions to address

1. Have you defined a clear strategic leadership positioning based on innovation, cost or customer experience?
2. Have you integrated SC in your business model at both the value proposition and at the operating system levels?
3. How have you linked your business strategy to your SC model?
4. Have you assessed the WTP of your customers?
5. Have you identified the complexity factors impacting the end-to-end SC cost?
6. Have you differentiated the complexity factors you control and the external ones you do not control?
7. Have you identified actions to simplify your supply chain?
8. How is your company positioned on the fair value model?
9. Have you developed actions to offer differentiated services to your customers in order to increase the WTP?
10. Do you consider SCM as a potential leverage of getting a competitive advantage?

# Chapter 11
# Control your supply chain performance

## Key ideas

### 1. Overall approach

Controlling the SC performance has to go through the following steps:

- Consider the five-parameter value equation model introduced in Chapter 1, which provides the value priorities, and then the relevant domains of performance objectives
- List the potential KPIs by value domain: customer satisfaction, OPEX, working capital, assets and sustainability
- Define the mathematical calculation of each KPI, which is a critical topic. For instance concerning OTIF, we have multiple ways of calculating it:
  By order line.
    - By order: this approach is much tougher than the previous. Imagine a customer order with three lines: the first two lines have been delivered OTIF but there is a missing piece for the last one. If you calculate OTIF by order line, the KPI will be 67% and by order the performance will be 0%. The perception of the performance will be very different for the same performance.
    - At the exit of your warehouse gate: we talk about shipped OTIF.
    - At the delivery gate of your customer's warehouse: we talk about delivered OTIF.
    - Even on the shelf in the supermarket in the brick and mortar retail model, and we introduced in the Part A introduction the notion of OSA as On Shelf Availability.
- Complete this list of KPIs by a list of key activity parameters, such as the volume of tonnes or in pallets, the number of orders, order lines, SKUs, delivery points, truck capacity load, etc. Those parameters have to be followed as explanatory factors of the potential economy of scale (positive leverage of performance) and of higher complexity (negative leverage of performance).

- Select a short list of KPIs you will be using on a regular basis.
- Consider the governance model, which defines accountability roles and missions in order to allocate the KPIs to the right stakeholders.
- Define the cosmetics presentation of the KPIs and the related information you want to share such as the objective, the YTD result, the YoY data, etc. This is a key topic in order to facilitate the visualisation, to detect deviation and to generate corrective actions.
- Formalise the process of:
    - Breaking down and cascading the aggregated KPI dedicated to the management team into the lower levels of the organisation.
    - Defining the KPI objectives (yearly, monthly, etc.).
    - Controlling (frequency).
    - Issuing the KPI itself based on elementary data generally from the ERP. This point can clearly be an issue.
    - Producing the KPI by using specific software extracting and forming the KPI.
    - Formalising the corrective action plan and the tracker of the outcome of such plan.

## 2. The structure of a SC dashboard

On the diagram 1, we introduce the template of an SC dashboard, which is structured around four chapters we consider quite relevant:

| Coefficient | Description | Target | Performance |
|---|---|---|---|
| 20 | OTIF | 85% | 86% |
| 40 | Global Key Accounts (GKA) OTIF | 93% | 82% |
| 15 | Customer complaint number for the month | 15 | 79% |
| 25 | Nb of GKA Customer complaints solved > 30 days YTD | 0% | 100% |
| 100 | Customer Perspective – What value should we add to customers? | | 86,85% |
| 20 | Sales forecast accuracy core products | 90% | 100% |
| 40 | Replenishment on time delivery performance | 85% | 100% |
| 40 | Stock coverage | 80% | 0% |
| 100 | Operational excellence perspective – What do we excel at? | | 60% |
| 25 | Value of inventories | 100% | 87% |
| 55 | Local supply chain costs | 95% | 100% |
| 20 | Overdues | 3% | 100% |
| 100 | Financial perspective - How do supply chains contribute to cost-cutting? | | 96,75% |
| 35 | TF1 accidents in logistics | 8 | 100% |
| 30 | Cost-to-serve savings targets (M€) | 8 | 100% |
| 25 | Packaging (pallets, rolls, etc.) (M€) | 2 | 100% |
| 10 | Rush orders | 3% | 0% |
| 100 | Development perspective – What progress are we achieving? | | 90,00% |

Diag. 1: Example of a SC dashboard

- The **value delivered to the customers**. In this case, four KPIs have been selected:
  - OTIF for all orders.
  - OTIF dedicated to the key accounts in order to track the delivered value to the global KA. This is a special request from the CEO of that company.
  - Number of customer complaints.
  - Lead-time to fix global key accounts complaints. This is again a special focus for the CEO.
- The **operational excellence** perspective of SCM:
  - The sales forecast accuracy measured by the standard deviation of the series of gaps between actual sales versus demand forecast. But interestingly, this forecast accuracy is followed only for the core products related to the AX products (see Part B introduction). The point is that, for AX products managed in MTS (Make-To-Stock) with a high level of OTIF promise, the demand forecast accuracy is absolutely critical.
  - The replenishment on-time delivery performance. In this company, the production plants are centralised and provide the products to the local sales organisations based in the countries. The idea is to control the reliability of the replenishment lead-time from the central plants to the local sales entities to secure the promise of order-to-delivery lead-time to customers.
  - The stock coverage of finished goods is the DIO introduced in Chapter 4 and measured in number of days of sales. There is no focus neither on raw material, which are commodities, nor on WIP, as the process of production is continuous.
- The **financial performance** of SCM with Chapter 9 and three KPIs are specifically followed:
  - Complementary to the value of inventories in M€, estimate the level of cash frozen in the working capital.
  - In supply chains generally the outbound logistics, which means the flow from the last stock location to the final customer counts for the biggest part of the total end-to-end SC cost. This is why this cost-to-serve or almost this last mile cost is under a special control. This cost, as explained in Chapter 3, depends on the level of service promised to the customer.
  - The last KPI is the overdue, representing the part of the DSO (days of sales outstanding), which doesn't respect the general sales terms included in the contract with the customers. This is another part of the working capital that has to be eliminated.

On diagram 2, another example of a company driven by finance has developed an SC financial dashboard quite comprehensively focusing on the global financial amounts by category of costs, but also analysing those costs by unit. As we mention with the key activity parameter, we can match the financial KPI with the volume, which is a quite important driver. In terms of types, it is interesting to note in that case the focus on:

- The global margin, in order to develop the awareness of the supply chain managers of their impact on gross margin.
- The overstock and the obsolescence due to the short life cycle of the products, the continuous launch of new products and the big part of the sales done through promotions.
- The demurrage costs in port waiting for the loading of the containers on the vessels. This cost can be the consequence of the lack of the planning synchronisation between the production plant and the transportation solution for such global companies managing flows at the intercontinental level.
- Finally, the customer service plays a critical role in the WTP of the customers and a lot of investments have been made in people, processes and tools. Therefore, there is a focus on the customer service cost.

| Global financial KPIs |
| --- |
| Invoiced units (in k Units) |
| Consolidated net sales (in M€) |
| Gross margin per unit (in €/unit) |
| COGS (in M€) |
| **Total SC costs (in M€)** |
| Inbound transportation costs (in M€) |
| Overstock and obsolete (in M€) |
| Logistics costs (in M€) |
| Outbound transportation costs (in M€) |
| Demurrage costs (in M€) |
| Customer service costs (in M€) |

| Total SC cost per invoiced unit (in €) |
| --- |
| Inbound costs per invoiced unit (in €) |
| Overstock and obsolete per invoiced unit (in €) |
| Logistics costs per invoiced unit (in €) |
| Outbound transportation costs per invoiced unit (in €) |
| Demurrage costs per invoiced unit (in €) |
| Customer service costs (in M€) |
| **Total SC cost (in % of gross margin)** |
| Inbound transportation costs (in % of GM) |
| Overstock and obsolete (in % of GM) |
| Logistics costs (in % of GM) |
| Outbound transportation costs (in % of GM) |
| Demurrage costs (in % of GM) |
| Customer service costs (in % of GM) |

Diag. 2: Focus on the financial SC KPIs

- The last chapter covers **transformation projects** related to innovative disruption or to incremental changes. In the example, the management team has decided to focus on the four following topics:
  - The safety measured by the TF1, which measures the number of accidents resulting in more than 24 hours of work disruption. Actually, in this company the safety is considered as a developing topic but in more advanced companies this kind of KPI is structural and belongs to a chapter on sustainability.
  - The savings related to the cost-to-serve after modelling the fair value (see Chapter 10).
  - The savings related to the packaging.
  - The rush orders as a potential indicator of a service problem occurrence. An increase of the rush order rate against the total number of orders, leading to a higher express transportation spent, can be the result of internal problems the company faces such as a lack of cooperation between production and sales, which is by essence an SCM topic.

A weight has been allocated to each chapter. Here in this case the chapters have an equal weight and within each chapter coefficients can be as well allocated to each KPI in order to have a global performance assessment of the SCM for the company.

## Take-away for leaders

The first recommendation is to have an SC dashboard reviewed on a monthly frequency by the management team. The SC performance relies on multiple players and it is key to involve them. The good place to use a KPI cockpit is the executive S&OP meeting (see Chapter 13).

There is in some business environment discussion about the use of the KPIs and some people even recommend not using them anymore in order to escape from the command and control management style. We believe in trust, empowerment and collaboration to generate performance, but we believe as well in metrics to put the operational excellence under control. The point is not to blame but to detect issues and improvement opportunities and collectively to make progress. As the most cross-functional process, SCM performance is by essence fragmented. The SCM performance relies on collective intelligence. The lack of SCM performance relies more at the interface of operations rather than on the individual ones.

An SC dashboard has to be designed according to the five-parameter value equation. Those KPIs have to be carefully selected and the size of the SC dashboard should fit onto an A4 page. Measuring is one compulsory thing in order to build up a fact-based platform shared within the management team. Of course the more important thing is to launch actions if the performance target is away from the objectives.

## Key questions to address

1. Do you have an SC dashboard shared at the management team level?
2. If yes, what are the regular actions you launch?
3. Have you linked your SC dashboard to incremental improvements?
4. Have you tested the consistency of your SC governance model with the performance objectives definition and with the allocation of the KPIs?
5. Is the SC dashboard generation fully integrated within the ERP?
6. Have you included financial SC KPIs?
7. Have you a clear corrective action process followed by a tracker of the action impact?
8. Have you implemented a glossary of SC KPIs within the overall company?
9. Do you use the SC dashboard in the executive S&OP meeting?
10. Have you a robust process dedicated to KPIs to link the management team to the operational teams in a top-down and bottom-up process?

# Chapter 12

# Segment your SC models to support specific business strategies

## Key ideas

The perspective of this book is to position SCM as a business leverage supporting the strategic ambition of a company. The purpose of this chapter is to propose a methodology to design concurrent SC models (see Chapter 10) for a given company managing a portfolio of different strategic segments.

## 1. Corporate strategy and SC models segmentation

The corporate strategy analyses the strategic consequences of a diversified portfolio of businesses. The development of strategic business units (SBU) is the organisational answer to the identification of strategic segments characterised by specific key success factors (KFS). Even if those businesses can share some common core activities such as R&D, purchasing and marketing through the branding for instance, they run activities in different competitive environment. In the following example, the segmentation based on products reveals different market situations in terms of maturity and growth, margin. Consequently, the key success factors are specific.

| Strategic segment | S1 | S2 | S3 |
|---|---|---|---|
| Products | Standard products | Trade products | Customized products for specific applications |
| Market | Low margin<br>Specialized and strong competition<br>Mature market<br>Market potential : + | Low margin<br>Specialized and strong competition<br>Mature market<br>Market potential : ++ | High margins<br>High competition<br>Growing market<br>Market potential : +++ |
| Key success factors | → High level of end-to-end customer centric Supply Chain : lead time reliability, quality and cost<br>→ Products standardisation<br>→ The fair value | → Customer intimacy and market knowledge<br>→ Market price<br>→ Product availability and related lead time | → Product reliability and performance (R&D)<br>→ Integration of design, production and tests<br>→ Innovation and time to market for new product |

Diag. 1: Example of Strategic Business units

In diagram 2, another company manages several activities organised in business units (BU) and a double mapping has been provided:

– The profitability growth versus the volume growth, which are key drivers of the SC design
– The application of the fair value model by matching the variable margin in $ per ton and the cost-to-serve with the same unit. It shows that the large BU1 and the small BU6, being above the diagonal, the SC provides a competitive advantage and the other BUs are aligned along the diagonal but with different value creation levels, which leads to potential more or less complex SC models.

Part B  Design and animate the right supply chain models to create a competitive advantage

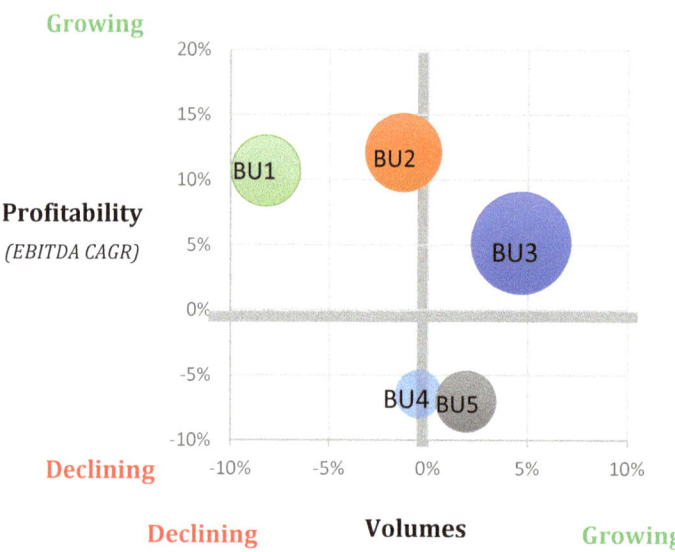

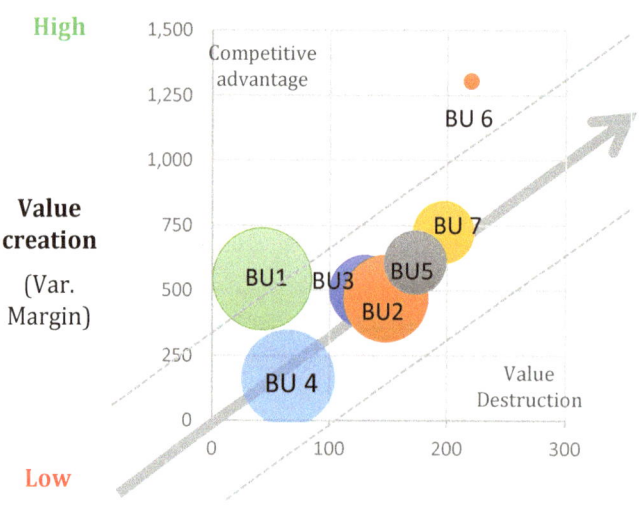

Diag. 2: Corporate strategy and strategic segmentation
(example from a manufacturing company in the chemical industry)

## 2. The segmentation variables

Beyond the strategic variables of segmentation based on growth and volumes, margin level and key success factors, which impact mostly the five-parameter value equation, we recommend using a set of complementary variables more oriented to test the opportunity of specialising the building blocks of the SC operating system. Those variables are categorised into three chapters and we propose a list of the main segmentation criteria:

- **Suppliers/production facilities:**
  - OTIF performance: the SC solutions have to consider the performance of the service level.
  - Location: the SC operating model will be different if the supplier's location is overseas, continental, regional, country-based or local.
  - Criticality: some suppliers have a weak service but for instance as a single source or as a vendor of a critical raw material or component, it is strategic to keep them, and then specific solutions have to be implemented to support them.
- **Products:** the ABC/XYZ/123 matrix we explained in the Part B introduction is a good basis for segmenting products and defining specific SC solutions. Other criteria can be used:
  - OTIF objective.
  - Volume: high vs low.
  - Demand pattern: volatility, trends and seasonality.
  - Value: high vs low.
  - Product life cycle: short vs long.
  - Shelf life: short vs long.
- **Customers/geographies:**
  - OTIF objective.
  - Volume.
  - Location.
  - Order profile: number of order line and volume per order line.

Those segmentation criteria impact the following building blocks of the SC operating system:

- Governance and allocation of accountabilities between central vs local entities.
- Planning strategies and decoupling positioning: MTS, MTO, MTS/MTO.
- Inventory dimensioning, especially the safety stock with pooling solutions.

- Industrial and logistics footprint: central, regional or local.
- Sourcing and production: one product produced in one plant (single sourcing) or one product produced in several plants (multi-sourcing).
- Shipment: direct, cross-dock and route-to-market structure: short or long.
- Automation: none, semi-automation or full.

Matching all those segmentation criteria can lead to a huge number of SC models. Finding out the right ones is the result of a dialogue closely involving the management team and the supply chain professionals in order to consider the most relevant strategic variables and to select the value equation and the building blocks of the operating system, which have to be specific.

Diagram 3 shows an example of a company in the construction industry, which has designed and implemented six different SC models to cope with the diversity of these situations. The main two segmentation criteria are:

- The different offers to customers and especially the order-to-delivery lead-time, which goes from immediate availability for the fast runners to 60 calendar days for highly customised products.
- The product profiles in terms of ABC/XYZ classification.

As a consequence, each SC model is characterised by:

- The order-to-delivery lead-time enabled by a given SC model.
- The route-to-market pattern, which goes through the upstream mass production plants, the logistics platforms and the downstream converting/finishing factory.
- The SC planning strategy, which can be MTS, MTS/MTO or even MTO and consequently the positioning of the inventories.

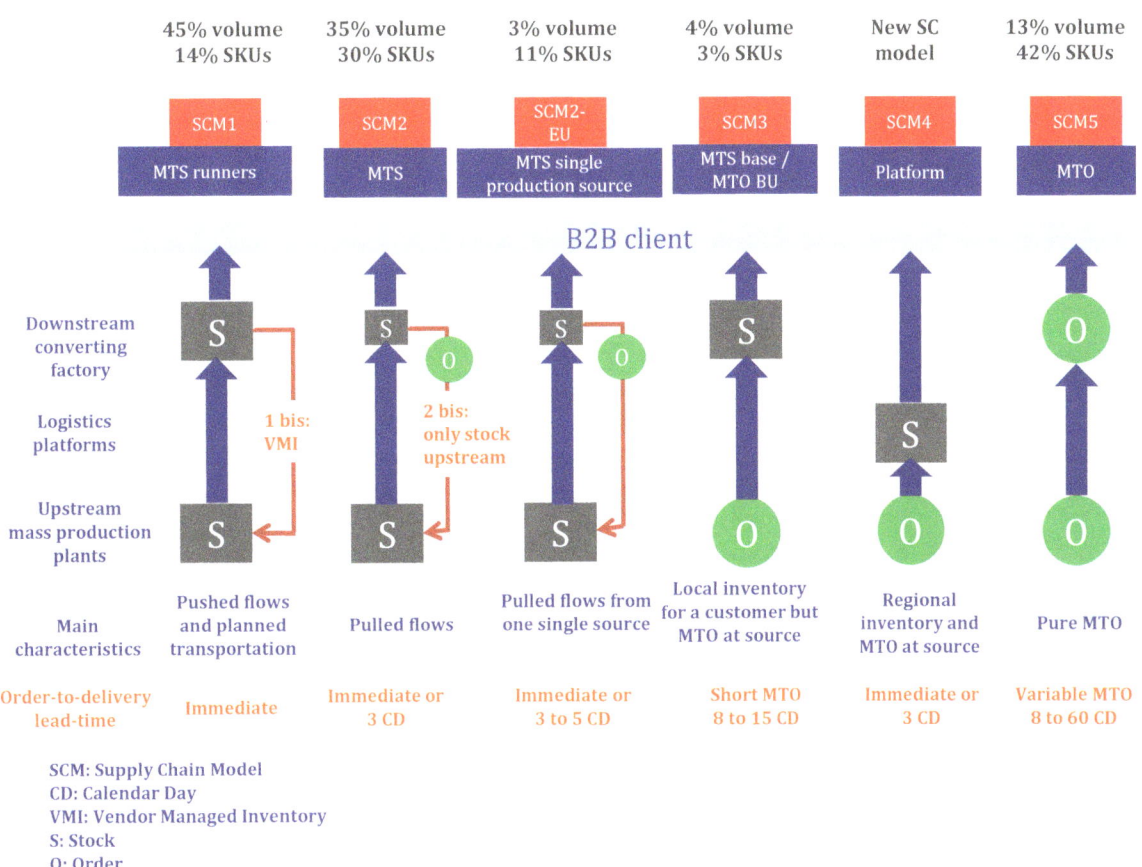

Diag. 3: Example of segmented SC models
(example from a manufacturing company in the construction industry)

The number of SKUs managed by this model and the volume characterises each SC model. The first two SC models involve a big part of the products and the volume. The four others concern far fewer products and lower volume but it enables the company to keep a growing market share and to get a competitive advantage by having SC models generating an overall higher performance due to specialisation.

## 3. The methodology to design SC model and to segment SC models

As explained in Chapter 10, the SC model derives from the strategy of the company and is composed of two main dimensions (see diagram 3):

- Out of the five-parameter value equation, we focus here on the customer offer made of products, solutions and services, as the main driver of an SC operating system. The main question to address is: 'What do we offer to our customers?'
- The SC operating system with a specific focus on the logistics system, the monitoring system and the governance system. Here the question is: 'Which solutions and means do we have to build up and to use in order to fulfil the customer offer?'

The + between those two dimensions reminds us that the SC operating system has to be aligned to the customer offers and respect the paradigm of fair value.

**STRATEGY**

### Supply chain model

| Customer offer | SC operating system |
|---|---|
| • Products<br>• Solutions (kits, systems, special products)<br>• Services (logistics and non-logistics services) | • Logistic system: from finished good sourcing to delivering to customer:<br>　• Physical road to market<br>　• Type of logistic infrastructure<br>　• Own logistic infrastructure or outsourced?<br>• Monitoring system:<br>　• Planning strategy<br>　• Inventory management model<br>• Governance system:<br>　• RACI for major processes |
| **What do we offer to customers ?** | **What solutions/means ?** |

Diag. 4: The components of a SC model

In a given market, we have to check if the core SC operating system is able or not to meet the different SC segments. According to the previous paragraph, we recommend using the following three main segmentation variables:

- The **customer profile** in terms of channel. The multi-channel and the omnichannel (see Chapter 14) have to be considered in B2B and B2C environments. DIY, supermarkets, grocery stores, on line store, market place, hypermarkets, cash and carry embed a potential diversity of customer expectations and then specific offers. According to this segmentation variable, N customer offers will be designed.
- The **product profile** based on the ABC/XYZ/123 matrix analysis (see Part B introduction).
- The **geography** of both suppliers and customers: local, regional or intercontinental.

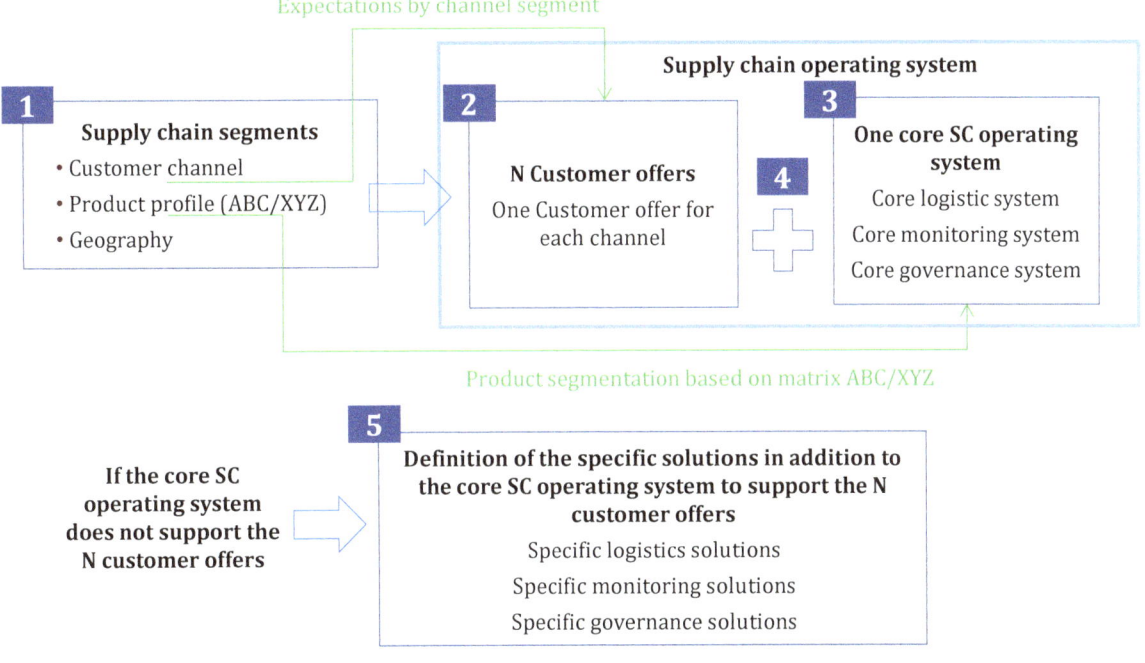

Diag. 5: SC segments and SC models

In order to design an appropriate SC model, we recommend from a methodological perspective managing in parallel two analyses, as follows (see diagram 6):

- On the **demand side**, the two segmentation variables we select are the customer channels and the geographies. Based on both those variables, customer channel expectations are formalised (step 1). Based on the customers' channels expectations, N channel segments are identified and matched with a generic customer offer (step 2). Each of them is characterised by a homogeneous customer offer and, based on segmentation, N customer offers are identified (step 3).
- On the **supply side** in parallel, one core SC operating system is designed and mostly driven by the product profile (ABC/XYZ) (step 1') and completed by the geographies of the suppliers (step 2'). This core SC operating system is described in its three main building blocks (step 3'):
  - The monitoring strategy in terms of MTS, MTO or MTS/MTO (see Part B introduction). This criterium has a fundamental impact on the supply lead-time: a MTS product generates stock by essence, and then the lead-time can be short whereas a MTO product has to be scheduled in production and leads to a longer lead-time.
  - The route-to-market (see Part A introduction), which links the suppliers to the customers. The location of the suppliers is the second major driver of the supply lead-time.
  - The governance system defining through a RACI methodology (see Chapter 9) accountabilities among the players.
- The reconciliation of the demand side with the supply side is done in steps 4 and 4'. This reconciliation is mostly done on the lead-times. The approach consists of matching the customer lead-time (the required order-to-delivery lead-time by customers) with the supplier lead-time, which depends on how the product is produced and where the supplier is located. There are two options:
  - If the generic SC operating system is able to meet each of the N customer offers, the job is done and this core SC operating system will not be changed.
  - If some customer offers cannot be served by the core SC operating model, therefore specific solutions have to be designed and to be implemented complementary to the core SC operating system in order to deliver all customer offers, and will generate several segmented SC models as displayed in diagram 3.

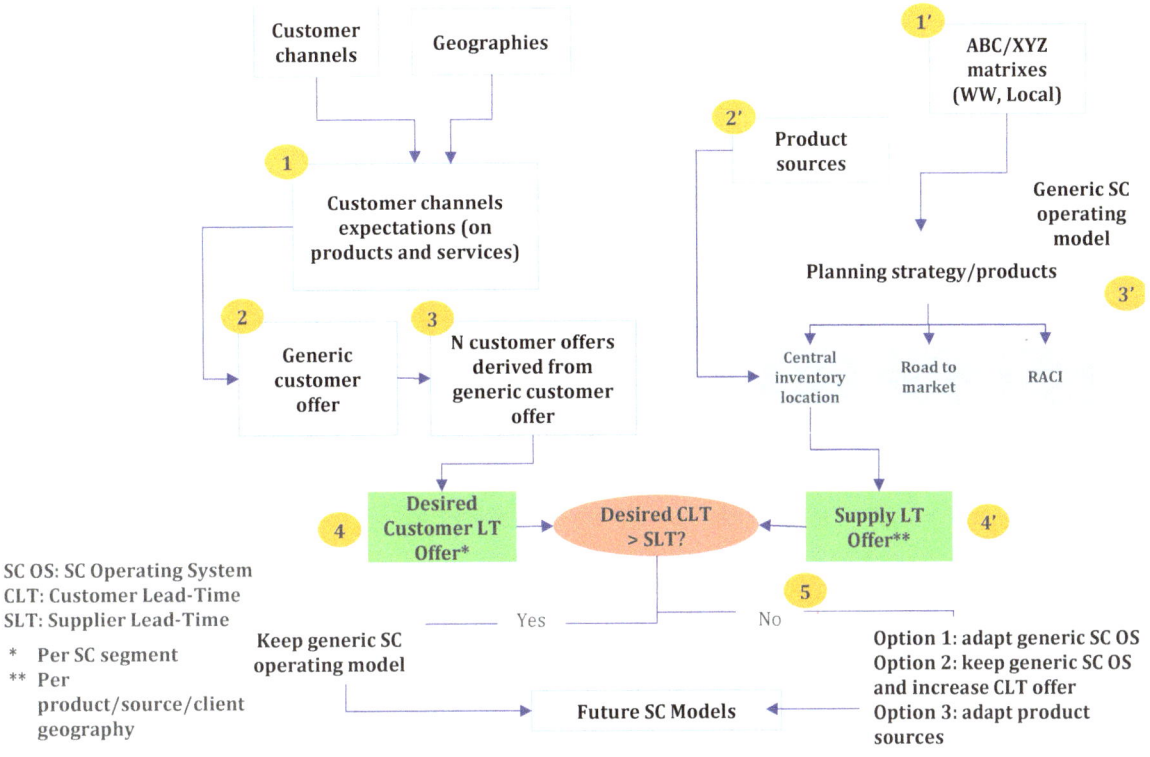

Diag. 6: Methodology overview for designing a SC model

## 4. The segmented SC models and the link to the fair value paradigm

In Chapter 10 we have introduced the second paradigm of SCM as fair value and we have given the example of a company that has decided to simplify its SC model in order to be more consistent with the WTP of its business and to get back to the fair value diagonal. We propose to use the same case study as follows:

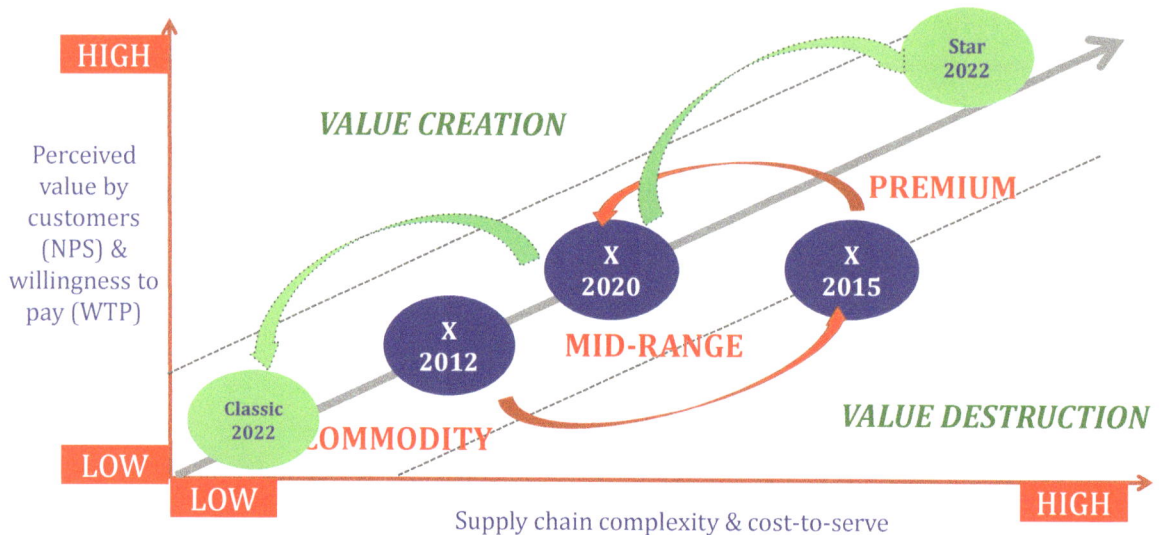

Diag. 7: Fair value and segmented SC models
(example from a manufacturing company in the construction industry)

Actually, to fine tune the SC model design, in this case, two strategic segments have been pointed out:

- The **star segment** is made of high-end products purchased by big customers through highly competitive tenders with strong penalties in case of delivery delay. The SC operating model is quite complex, based on MTO planning strategy even for very specific case ETO (Engineer-To-Order) (see Chapter 9 for the governance of the demand planning process), a single source of production, which leads to a sophisticated logistics route-to-market and customer service plays a critical role as this is project-based business and solutions have to be designed according to the specification of the customer. The three steps of the customer relationship – pre-sales, sales and after sales – have to be under a tight control for this customer service. This SC model is more a global-to-global model (see Part A introduction).
- The **classic segment** is made of commodities products with large volumes and lower margin. The SC model has to be simple and lean as the WTP is by essence quite low. It will be a local-to-local SC pattern to minimise the end-to-end SC cost based on a short route-to-market. The customer service could be automatised through a digital marketplace in order to speed up the transactional lead-time and to lower the interface cost with the customers.

# Testimony from Andros

Florian DELMAS, CEO, Andros.

Jérôme RIO, Supply Chain Managing Director, Andros.

*Could you introduce Andros in terms of strategic market positioning?*

Andros is a multi-local player in the agro-food industry acting in the transformed fruit, desserts and testy yogurts market. We offer a large range of products by addressing the mass-retail markets through our own brands and as well through private labels, but away-from-home and industrial players markets. That means six major distribution channels supported by a dense and varied product portfolio. We have strong market positions in France, in Europe, in the US and in Asia through a controlled-temperature network (from 11 to 90 days of shelf life), dry products and frozen products (up to 24 months of shelf life).

A specific dimension of our business model is to have integrated the value chain from the sourcing of the fruit-based upstream, the transformation of those fresh raw fruits, their storage and the final transformation within our assembly and packaging plants. Consequently, our supply chain is quite integrated.

*What is the scope of supply chain management within Andros?*

The supply chain goes through the full organisation. Therefore, supply chain is a great enabler to align the teams at the cultural and operational levels, supported by a set of tools in order to continuously serve our customers.

In order to achieve that, we have dedicated supply chain teams at each level of our organisation from the strategic to the operational level with clear formalised missions. Our supply chain processes are supported by both powerful information technology-based tools (forecasting, under constraint planning, scheduling, stock management, logistics information system) and facilities-based tools such as warehouses we manage in house or with Third Party Logistics. The roll out of those solutions is a continuous journey.

***What is the expected value supply chain management accountable for in order to support the business strategy?***

Pragmatism is our main driver. It depends on multiple variables such as the market segment, the own brands or private labels, and the supply chain trade-offs may vary according to our strategic choices and objectives. But nevertheless, one value is our priority: customer satisfaction in terms of both product and service quality, and fulfilment for our customers and the consumers.

The strategic stakes vary according to the constraints of our different business models. For instance, Covid-19 will have been an outstanding learning experience of adjustment and flexibility with an unprecedented background so far in terms of rebalancing a huge volume from the away-from-home channel to the mass-retail channel. This big shift obliged us to reengineer somehow the end-to-end chain from the sourcing, the transformation, the storage and to the final distribution.

***Do you believe supply chain management creates a competitive advantage?***

The large content and the diversity of our product portfolio eventually drive our supply chain as a key-differentiating factor for the business. Product quality, service to customers, management of our manufacturing assets and cash management are the axes of that differentiation. As mentioned before this is particularly true as we have integrated the value chain along from the fresh fruits to the finished products sold to a large diversity of customers.

***You manage a diversified portfolio of products and of customers. Consequently, do you have developed parallel supply chain models?***

Our multi-local model combined with the diversity of our product offer pushes us to a pragmatic approach in terms of supply chain models. The key driver is the lead-time in terms of product shelf life as mentioned in the first question. This parameter matched with our facilities footprint has strongly driven the development of our supply chain models. The shorter the lead-time is, the more the local-to-local supply chain model has been developed. This local-to-local model impacts the manufacturing system and also the monitoring of the supply chain, which can be located at the plant level. By contrast, we have some products that are manufactured on a single plant and delivered in more than 100 countries throughout the world. In that case, the supply chain model is mainly a local-to-global one.

*What are the main projects in the supply chain domains you are working on?*

The main projects belong to two main categories. The first one entails organisational projects such as the implementation of the S&OP processes and the numerous related transformation projects (cost-to-serve, safety stock policy, inventory deployment policy, etc.). On the other hand, we have launched IT projects in order to provide the tools to support those changes. Our ability to make the best decision as soon as possible based on real data is a major stake of our transformation. The company is engaged in a digitalisation journey (modelling, analytics and connectivity) focused on both tactical and operational processes in order to support our organisational transformation with the required agility.

## Take-away for leaders

In a company that manages a portfolio of activities, specialising the SC models according to the specific strategic characteristics of each business a company competes in enables them to better serve the competitive drivers of each activity.

Therefore, the five-parameter value equation can be adapted to each business according to its key success factors. We recommend challenging the common five-parameter value equation of the whole company and segmenting it if a specific value has to be generated according to the strategy of a given business.

Consequently, in a second step, as explained in Chapter 10, the SC operating system can be customised too. But there is a trade-off to consider between specialising the solutions of each SC operating system versus keeping some solutions common and shared between each BU-based operating system, which enables us to keep economies of scale, a major stake. Leaders have to make arbitration between differentiation vs consolidation in terms of SC models.

We recommend having a maximum number of seven SC models to avoid complexity and to keep a minimum level of shared solutions generating economies of scale.

The fair value model introduced in Chapter 10 is quite useful to validate a relevant segmentation in terms of the strategy of value positioning through the competitive advantage lens and the implementation of different specific SC operating models.

## Key questions to address

1. Do you consider competing in different strategic segments characterised by different key success factors?
2. Would it make sense to have in your company two or more five-parameter value equations?
3. In terms of SC model pattern (see Part A introduction) do you have a single one or several?
4. What are the main building blocks of the SC operating model, which have to be specific according to a specific value equation?
5. What are the main building blocks of the SC operating model, which have to be common whatever a differentiation strategy may be?
6. What are the most relevant criteria of segmentation of your SC models: the value equation, the characteristics of your suppliers, products or customers?
7. Do you have a big diversity of your products value and margin?
8. Do you have a big diversity of business growth?
9. Do you use mathematical models to simulate and to estimate the relevance of segmenting your SC models?
10. Have you used the fair value model to test the robustness of the SC model segmentation?

# Chapter 13

# Be agile and build One Team through IBP (Integrated Business Planning)

## Key ideas

S&OP/IBP is the backbone of SCM. There are two terminologies to name this tactical cross-functional process, which is related to the maturity of the process.

### 1. Positioning of S&OP/IBP within SC planning

Diagram 1 displays the different layers of a multi-level planning. We differentiate generally between three planning levels completed by an execution one:

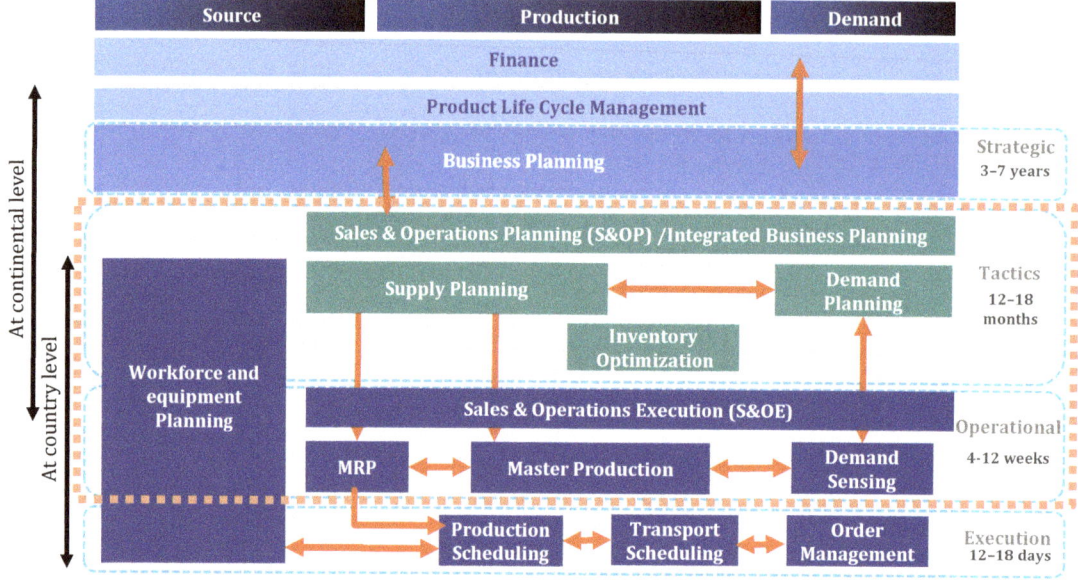

Diag. 1: Overview of SC planning

- The **strategic level,** which runs for 3–7 years according to the industry. SCM essentially plays a role for designing the right SC model based on the footprint of logistics and manufacturing facilities with the dimensioning of the related capacities. This CAPEX part is crucial as this plan focuses on both organic and external growth. The name of this yearly process can be a Strategic and Financial Plan and it includes the strategic product plan.
- The **tactical level** supported by S&OP. The horizon of this monthly rolling planning exercise in terms of the state of the art is 18 months in order to get some visibility beyond the budget. This plan is done at both central and local (country) levels.

The following table provides an example of the nature of the topics that are covered by those two planning levels and the types of decisions that have to be made. This is an example of an industry for which the customer, as in automotive or aircraft industries, certifies the production tooling:

|  | **Decisions** | **Drivers and constraints** |
|---|---|---|
| **18 months and more** | • Industrial and logistics investments with new footprint | • Necessary time to build an investment file: 12–18 months |
|  | • New investments ramp up | • Machine efficiency during ramp up |
|  | • New product allocation to production sites | • Site validation by customers: 6 months |
|  | • Actual production reallocation to new plant | • Site validation by customers: 6 months<br>• Saturation of all critical business resources |
|  | • Decisions of capacity allocation to markets | • Economical arbitration between revenue/stock/costs |
| **2 months – 18 months** | • Load balancing between plants to saturate critical resources | • Transfer validation by customers: 6 months<br>• Transfer decisions with validation: between 1–2 months |
|  | • Capacity evolution to adjust to market evolutions (number of shifts, hours worked, etc.) | • 2 months for upstream production because of HR constraints<br>• Flexibility for post-manufacturing operations |
|  | • Inventory level optimization | • Campaign size<br>• Economical arbitration between revenue/stock/costs |
|  | • Arbitration on SKUs that are active on market | • Economical arbitration between revenue/stock/costs |

Table 1: Types of decisions impacting supply chain at strategic and tactical levels

– The **operational level** working on a 4–12 weeks horizon translates the decisions made from the S&OP process and is rolled out at the site level (local sales teams, production plants, logistics warehouses). The demand-sensing process enables us to update the tactical demand planning and the recommendation is to use the same date source channels and the same product structure (SKU, sub-family, family, S&OP aggregate, product line) in order to keep a high level of consistency.

A learnt lesson from the Covid-19 crisis is the benefit of closely connecting the tactical and the operational plans at the central level. With a high level of volatility and uncertainty, making supply–demand decisions more frequently (twice a month or even weekly instead of once a month) with a shorter planning horizon is critical and provides higher agility. We envision a future tendency to apply the S&OP principles to the operational horizon in order to support short-term trade-offs through an S&OE (Sales & Operations Execution).

## 2. The phases of the S&OP process

Diagram 2 displays the five steps of the S&OP:

Diag. 2: The decision cycle of IBP

- The entry point of the S&OP process is the **strategic plan**, which includes the growth ambition with the market share target, the development of products and upstream and downstream partnerships, the M&A plan, the key financial objectives in terms of margins, cash and profitability. It is at this step that the **arbitration rules** have to be formalised as a consequence of the strategic priorities.
- The second phase is the **demand review**. This phase is highly critical and the quality of this step drives the further steps of S&OP. The outcome of this phase is to generate an unconstrained demand plan and this is why this phase has to involve only people from sales and marketing teams and nobody from production, purchasing or finance. The main steps of that phase are to:
  - Analyse the demand pattern: trend, seasonality and volatility.
  - Analyse the past forecast performance.
  - Analyse the macro-economic including government regulations evolution, which could impact the demand.
  - Review the past actual sales.
  - Review the product plan.
  - Formalise the **assumptions** and the demand scenarios based on upside, downside and realistic assumptions.
  - Generate a validated unconstrained demand plan.
- The third phase is the **production and supply review**. Its purpose is to translate the demand plan into a purchasing plan and a production plan. As a result, if there is a problem of supply–demand mismatch, the unconstrained demand plan becomes a constrained sales plan. The main steps are to:
  - Analyse past production performance, especially through production adherence.
  - Review the potential supply and production problems such as production capacity, people absenteeism, sourcing shortage, production maintenance.
  - Propose demand plan change for meeting the available capacities.
  - Generate **supply plan, production and inventory plans** according to a proposed sales plan.
- The fourth phase is the **integrated reconciliation**. Integrated means collaborative, and its objective is to get a common single plan meeting both demand and supply objectives through the following activities:
  - Share supply issues and alternative solutions. Where there are constraints, potential shortages are shared and commercial priorities are given by marketing and sales.
  - Make decisions to balance demand and supply.
  - Identify areas of disagreement and further decisions through an escalation are required.

- Evaluate the **financial consequences** of the proposed plans.
- Prepare different financialised scenarios of S&OP plans (sales, supply, inventory).
– The fifth and last phase is the **executive S&OP meeting**, which has the purpose of **arbitrating conflicts** that were unfixed in the previous integrated reconciliation. The GM, who is the owner of the S&OP process, chairs this management team meeting. The agenda can be the following:
  - Review the key performance indicators.
  - Review future market trend and assumptions.
  - Aggregate-by-aggregate review.
  - New product update.
  - Collective impact on business plan.
  - Special issues.
  - Recap decisions.
  - Critique of the process.

## 3. The principles of the S&OP process

We consider that the S&OP process should respect the seven following principles:

a. The general manager of the company is the owner of that process. In other words, S&OP is a business process and the role of the SC manager is to facilitate it. The ultimate value of that process is to make arbitration between conflicts and the only person who has the holistic view and works strategically for the general interest of the company is the GM.
b. All stakeholders have to be involved, including HR as some decisions (number of shifts, temporary workers, etc.) have an HR impact.
c. S&OP is a tactical process meaning that the state-of-the-art horizon of planning is 18 months to have the visibility on the on-going budget and a view beyond it. In S&OP meetings we discuss tactical issues and not operational ones.
d. Performance is a focus point of S&OP and therefore a selective comprehensive set of KPIs has to be designed and reviewed on a monthly basis.
e. There is no S&OP and IBP without finance. Making arbitration decisions has to be based not only on volume data but on financial metrics (see Chapter 8).
f. Those arbitrations have to be done according to a set of formal, shared and clear rules. This is a fundamental basis of trust within the management team and the worst case is to base such arbitrations on discretionary elements, which destroy trust and don't support the strategic plan.

g. The last principle is to ensure consistency between the three plans of S&OP (sales, inventories and production) and the operational plans at the site level (sales regions, warehouses, plants). The S&OP decisions have to be understood and executed by the operational. If not, this process has no value.

## 4. IBP: a leverage of agility

IBP is about planning and we could think that the key words of IBP are: discipline, plans based on objectives definition, process and rules. This is true, but we do believe that IBP actually hybrids a mechanist approach with an organic one. In other words, IBP is a perfect ambidextrous leverage of exploitation (for instance optimising the margin under the capacity constraints) and exploration (finding out new sources of revenues to boost the revenue and use the available production capacity).

The following table shows for a series of attributes in which IBP embeds both mechanist and organic characteristics:

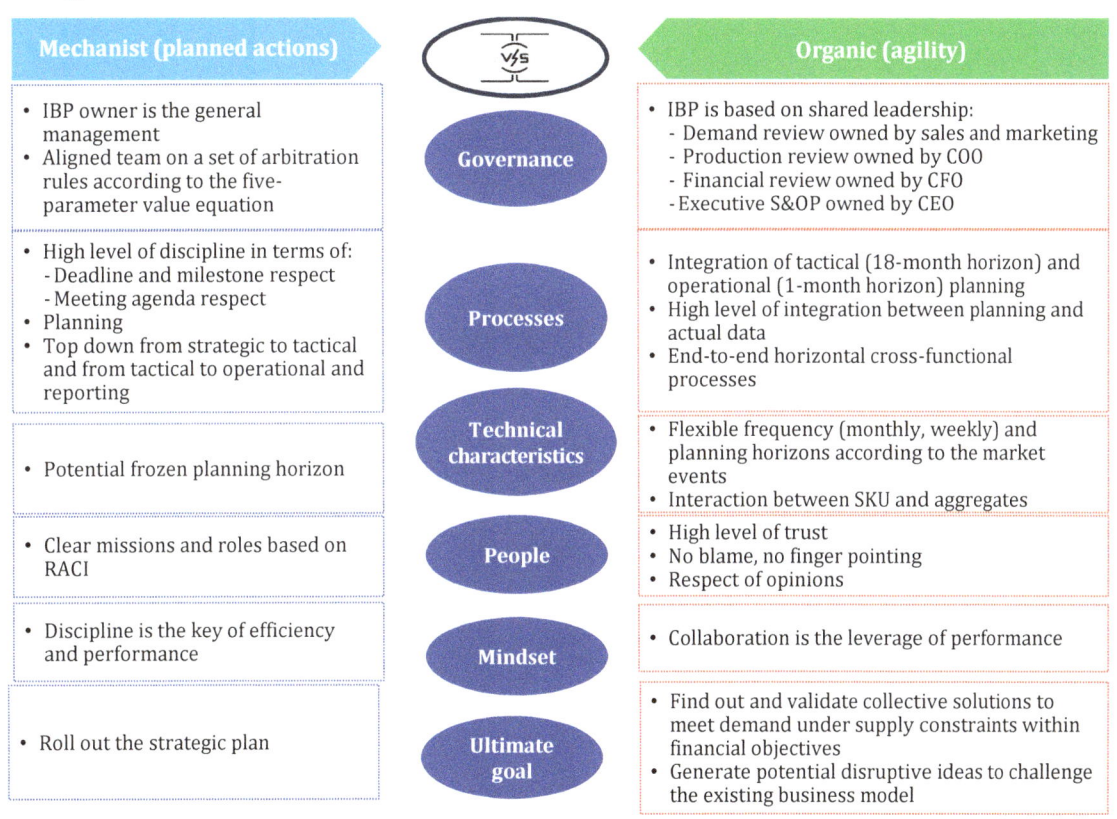

Table 2: The mechanist and the organic characteristics of IBP

## 5. IBP versus S&OP, axes of simplification and golden rules

### a) IBP versus S&OP

As we have mentioned, IBP is a more advanced S&OP characterised by:

- Greater financial integration.
- Inclusion of strategic initiatives and activities.
- Improved simulation and modelling.
- Easier interaction between detailed and aggregated information.
- Improved decision-making.
- Improved trust within the management team.

### b) Axes of simplification

It is important to apply the fair value paradigm to the S&OP and to keep it as simple as possible. We recommend some opportunities of simplification:

- The planning horizon can be 6 months at the beginning of the S&OP implementation, and then you can move on to 12 months to get at least the budget visibility.
- The frequency has to be flexible. If the market doesn't face too much fluctuation or if the business is based on yearly contracts, a quarterly frequency can be enough. As already mentioned, the opposite is true: if the uncertainty and the volatility increase a higher frequency can be appropriate.
- We recommend a roll-out without financial data and then, after at least one year when some routines are in place, integrating the financials.
- If you decide to apply a 24-month horizon, the first year data can be detailed at a monthly bucket and the second year at a quarterly bucket.
- It is not necessary to have a full scope covering all products, all markets, all geographies. This is preferable to start small by scoping the S&OP on the most critical parts of the business (products with potential shortage or high OTIF target, risky raw materials or components, production processes with bottlenecks, etc.).

## c) Golden rules of a successful implemented S&OP

As a summary we propose the following golden rules:

- Four building blocks have to be addressed in the process design of S&OP:
  - People: attitudes and competences.
  - Governance: accountability definition and arbitration rules.
  - Process: input data, tasks, reviews and output data.
  - Data and IT.
- Accountability of the GM for arbitration at the S&OP executive meeting.
- Clear and formal roles and missions of all stakeholders.
- Simulation of scenarios for preparing arbitrations.
- Common language based on a clear terminology.
- Discipline for rolling out the process.
- Have quality communication tools (template, tables, graphs) to facilitate the capture of the information, the conversation and the decision.
- Ensure a tangible outcome for all stakeholders.
- Beyond technical data, financials are crucial.
- Don't hesitate to simplify the S&OP state-of-the art to your organisation.
- Start small and learn by doing.
- Implementing S&OP takes time as building trust takes time, and the mid-term support of the GM is key to secure a success.

# Testimony from CertainTeed

Matt MADEKSZA, President, CertainTeed Insulation Group (until 31/01/2019); President, CertainTeed Roofing Group (since 31/01/2019)

Gonzalo LOPEZ-POLIN, Director of Supply Chain, CertainTeed Insulation Group

*Can you introduce the business of CertainTeed Insulation?*

CertainTeed aspires to be North America's recognised leader in sustainable habitat.

Through the responsible development of innovative and sustainable building products, CertainTeed has helped shape the building products industry for more than 110 years. Today CertainTeed® is North America's leading brand of exterior and interior building products, including roofing, siding, fence, decking, railing, trim, insulation, gypsum and ceilings. A subsidiary of Saint-Gobain, one of the world's largest and oldest building products companies, CertainTeed and its affiliates have more than 6,300 employees and more than 60 manufacturing facilities throughout the United States and Canada.

Sustainability has long been a part of CertainTeed's value system and corporate culture. CertainTeed takes pride in providing the best products to meet today's market needs, but also looking ahead to offer our customers innovations for tomorrow. CertainTeed focuses on offering high performing, affordable products that enhance users' comfort and wellbeing while reducing overall environmental impacts.

More specifically, CertainTeed Insulation believes in complete comfort, where your insulation system successfully controls thermal performance, air tightness, moisture management, and acoustics. That's why it offers a complete line of high-performance insulation products that work together to ensure every building achieves complete comfort.

*What are the main business challenges?*

There were several business challenges in 2017: selling price was too low across the board and there was also significant opportunity for customer and regional mix optimisation. Also some product lines were not financially sustainable and needed to be stopped.

In addition, product offer was way too large which led to inefficiencies across the entire supply chain, many costly services were provided to the customer at no cost, and freight was offered at a significant below-market rate.

Moreover, manufacturing performance was at poor levels and the business was known in the market for its constant quality problems.

The company was therefore facing critical challenges and was in need of a radical turnaround. Supply chain management optimisation has been a strategic enabler to make that possible.

### What is your vision of business value creation through supply chain management?

Achieving the best possible cost-effective model through a simplified and leaner product offer and logistics footprint, focusing on what actually delivers value to the customer to ensure we meet that new promise to the market. And all of this combined with a responsive and aligned organisation that handles the tactical dimension of the business based on a clearly defined, agreed and formalised process: the S&OP.

### What are the main actions you have implemented to generate such expected value?

Alignment of the exec team and questioning the existing status quo and mindset was the first challenge. Addressing it was a necessary first step to make possible all the changes that occurred after, and not only for supply chain-related topics.

Just after that, the most immediate key action, which delivered almost instant results, was the simplification of our product offer to the market and the revisiting of our customer lead-times based on what the customer was actually willing to pay for – *offering just enough* – and then the adherence to it – *no means no*. This was not as easy as it seems and required the involvement of all the key people of the company. It was a good initial exercise to start breaking the silos.

The other main action was the S&OP process implementation as the way to handle the tactical dimension of the business, involving all departments within the organisation.

Also, several initiatives were launched aiming at optimising and aligning the key processes within the areas of planning, transportation, warehousing and customer service.

***What are the benefits of S&OP you have implemented?***

Basically, making the best possible short and mid-term decisions – within the 3 to 12-month horizon range – in an effective and efficient manner and considering all scenarios and financial implications, as well as informing and engaging all the stakeholders along the entire process in a coordinated manner.

***What are the main results of the supply chain excellence program?***

Significant reduction of inventory levels required to maintain expected customer lead-times – main product family lines required inventory levels dropped by an average of 5 days on hand. Then manufacturing cost decreased thanks to a significant reduction in production changeovers. Also, a process put in place to proactively deal with product obsolescence significantly contributed to its mitigation. As a result of all of this combined with specific product storage optimisation initiatives, two external warehouses were closed leading to significant savings. In addition, we no longer have packaging stock outs leading to production line stops – which were previously frequent.

In addition, a great number of ancillary services entailing significant costs for the company are now being passed on to the customer. Also, a massive freight costs reduction has been achieved through our logistics footprint optimisation.

And last but not least, now the team has time to focus on further improvement actions opposed to daily firefighting. Continuous improvement is now a key element within our culture in supply chain.

## Take-away for leaders

Implementing and running an IBP process enables the management team to generate six valuable benefits:

- **Link the strategic plan to the operations.** Through the S&OP, SCM appears as a perfect leverage to cascade down the strategic decisions within the organisation, to take into consideration the market events from both supply and demand sides and to evaluate how operations perform those strategic objectives through a bottom-up process.

- Monitor the business in terms of ensuring the supply side of the supply chain will be meeting the demand side expectations, and if not make clear and shared arbitrations. The Covid-19 crisis has reinforced the need for a closer integration of the tactical and operational planning by linking S&OP and S&OE. Through this integration, the companies can be much more agile to face uncertainty. The objective of IBP is to detect risks, opportunities and constraints and to find out collective solutions. **IBP is the perfect process to balance planned actions (ex ante consistency) and agile decisions (ex post convergence).**

- Beyond the demand–supply balance, one take-away of the IBP is to **challenge the top line** and to detect opportunities of additional sales.

- Another dimension is to develop **predictability** by modelling uncertainty through what-if scenarios and to detect **risks** and to prepare mitigation actions or even **business continuity plans.**

- Monitor as well the business in terms of **financial management**. Through the financialisation of the IBP, the budgets can be managed more accurately and a significant improvement consists of making decisions on margins. Cost-to-serve, smart pricing and margins are key parameters of IBP (see Chapter 8). The following table summarises the financial benefits from IBP across four dimensions:

|  | **Variable Margin** *Decision Levers* | **Operating Expenses** *Decision Levers* | **Working Capital Employed** *Decision Levers* | **Fixed Capital Employed** *Decision Levers* |
|---|---|---|---|---|
| **Main levers** | ✓ Demand shaping (changes in product & customer mix)<br>✓ Market share growth through disciplined demand shaping strategies | ✓ Cost-to-serve through global SC management<br>✓ Better changeover/ campaign/ turnaround planning | ✓ Healthy inventory levels to support demand<br>✓ Specific inventory targets for each product family | ✓ Asset utilisation (OEE) and ROI<br>✓ Trade-off between seasonal stock and additional capacity |
| **Complementary levers** | ✓ Optimized pricing strategy based on volumes/price elasticity and anticipated raw materials trends<br>✓ Customer allocation strategies maximising profit | ✓ Reduced shipping costs: more stable plans, less firefighting<br>✓ Reduced external warehousing expenses for facing peak stocks | ✓ Safety stock dimensioning according to the potential risks of demand and supply sides<br>✓ Reduction of SLOB (slow movers and obsolete) | ✓ More optimised maintenance planning |

Table 3: The financial benefits of IBP

- Build up and reinforce your management team to get a more united **One Team**. IBP reveals normal objective conflicts among a management team and IBP through the arbitration process provides answers to those conflicts by aligning the team around a common goal based on the five-parameter value equation.

## Key questions to address

1. Do you have a clear mapping of your supply chain planning processes differentiating the strategic, tactical and operational levels?
2. Have you mapped the main decisions you make at each level of the supply chain planning system?
3. How could you evaluate the collective intelligence of your management team?
4. Do you regularly face conflicts between some stakeholders of your management team?
5. Have you formalised arbitration rules to fix conflicts?
6. Have you a process to formalise the assumptions related to the demand?
7. Do you build up upside, downside, realistic scenarios of the market demand?
8. How engaged is the general manager in the S&OP?
9. Have you financialised the S&OP?
10. Do you provide on a regular basis what-if scenarios?

# Chapter 14
# Use SCM to transform your company

## Key ideas

### 1. The drivers of the transformation

In Chapter 10, we introduced the five mega-drivers motivating a SC transformation.

**#1 Consumers**
Sophistication of expectations
Volatility

**#2 Patterns of consuming and retailing**
Omnichannel
Higher complexity

**#3 Changing geopolitical dynamics**
Stability
Regulation including tax
Footprint evolution and new routes

**#4 Technological innovations**
Smart automation
Connectivity
Data analytics

**#5 People**
New generations
Mobile work
Jobs: risks and opportunities
New forms of leadership

Diag.1: The drivers of the transformation

The consequences on the SC model are in general terms to move from an SC model driven by production planning and logistics to a SC model driven by customer centricity and business value creation. The five major evolutions are listed in the following diagram:

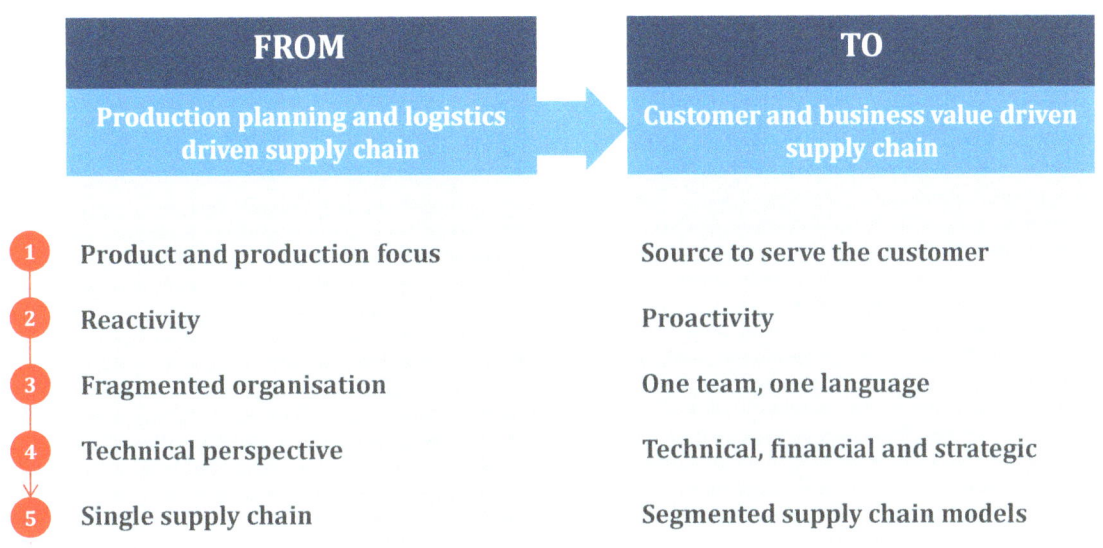

Diag.2: The potential breakthrough in supply chain management

We recognise the main potential leverages to reach such shift:

- An end-to-end seamless supply chain.
- An event-based monitoring approach.
- The S&OP/IBP enabling to boost the collaborative spirit of the company by developing One Team.
- The financialisaton of the supply chain.
- The development of concurrent SC models.

## 2. Challenge your business model: explore potential disruptive innovations

The historical link of SCM to operations has put improvement generation and even value creation in the way of incremental actions essentially driven by the achievement of a higher efficiency (getting a higher outcome with fewer resources). Most innovations in SC have been done in a step-by-step process supported by a change management approach, and breakthroughs were done only in a crisis case. Here we have selected four topics that we consider disruptive and that will generate a positive value.

## a) Challenge the value proposition to the market

The following diagram displays the Pareto analysis of the customers' portfolio of an industrial company selling cosmetics products in a given country in Europe. Each red square is the cost-to-serve for a specific customer measured as the % of the revenue generated by this customer. When we match the revenue with the cost-to-serve, we expect the following correlation: the higher the revenue is, the lower the cost-to-serve should be. This is obviously not the case. There are two potential reasons:

- The cost-to-serve in that country is not under control. Sales managers are motivated to sell a volume without considering the margin and the cost.
- After volume, the second driver of a cost-to-serve is the service delivered to the customer. The higher the level of service is, the more expensive the delivery cost is.

This is probably what happens here:

- The first three customers follow the correlation rule but then for the customer five the cost-to-serve is much lower than expected and the reason is likely grounded on the frequency of the deliveries (see Chapter 2)
- Customer nine generates a very high cost, actually the highest cost of the customer panel. For sure, the company has a special offer to that customer in terms of delivery frequency, specific packaging, free samples or express delivery lead-time.

This example shows that the first transformation a company has to do is to challenge its offer to its customers in coherence with the WTP of those customers (see Chapter 10) and the cost-to-serve. This transformation can be considered as disruptive as marketing and sales managers have to proactively accept to challenge their habits with their customers and to add to the sales volume objectives a gross margin.

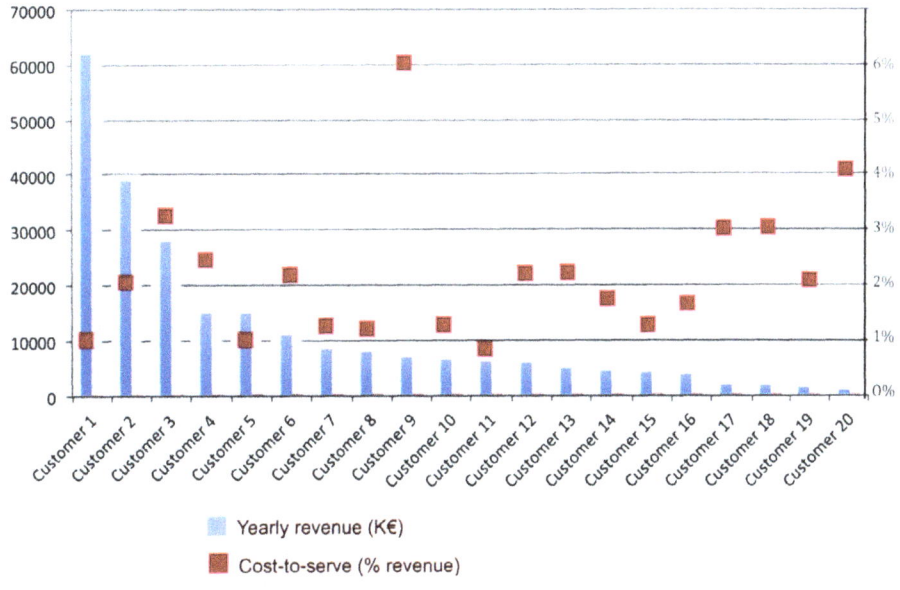

Diag.3: Cost-to-serve by customer profile

The development of an omnichannel commercial strategy is another axis of disruption for the value proposition of a company, especially by merging their B2B and B2C activities.

## b) Disrupt the SC operating system

Another domain of disruption involved the SC operating system. Diagram 4 shows the link of the SC cost to the OTIF. Each curve shows as in the previous example that the higher the OTIF is, the higher the SC cost. The bad news is that correlation is not linear but exponential. This is the first take-away of that diagram.

Model 1 (the red one) is the existing SC network, which is based on DC (distribution centre). The higher the number of DCs is, the higher OTIF, as the delivery lead-time is shorter to serve customers thanks to the shorter distance from the storage location to the customers' sites. But the higher the number of DCs is, the more expensive the SC cost is, because of the increased inbound transportation costs due to the fragmentation of the volumes, the real estate fixed costs and the inventory levels, which are not sufficiently counterbalanced by the presupposed outbound transportation cost decrease. If you keep model 1 in place, the only way to reduce the SC cost is to downgrade the service level to the customers by reducing the number of DCs through consolidation of flows.

Part B Design and animate the right supply chain models to create a competitive advantage

If you want to get significant SC costs savings by keeping the same OTIF, you have no choice: you have to disrupt your SC network model, for instance by shifting from the red model 1 to the black model 2. This model 2 is not based on DCs but on logistics platforms (PF), through which products are cross-docked and not stored. Model 2 provides the same benefits in terms of proximity to the customers but with a much lower cost thanks to the lighter profile of the involved logistics real estate and the absence of inventories as products are just dispatched through the platforms.

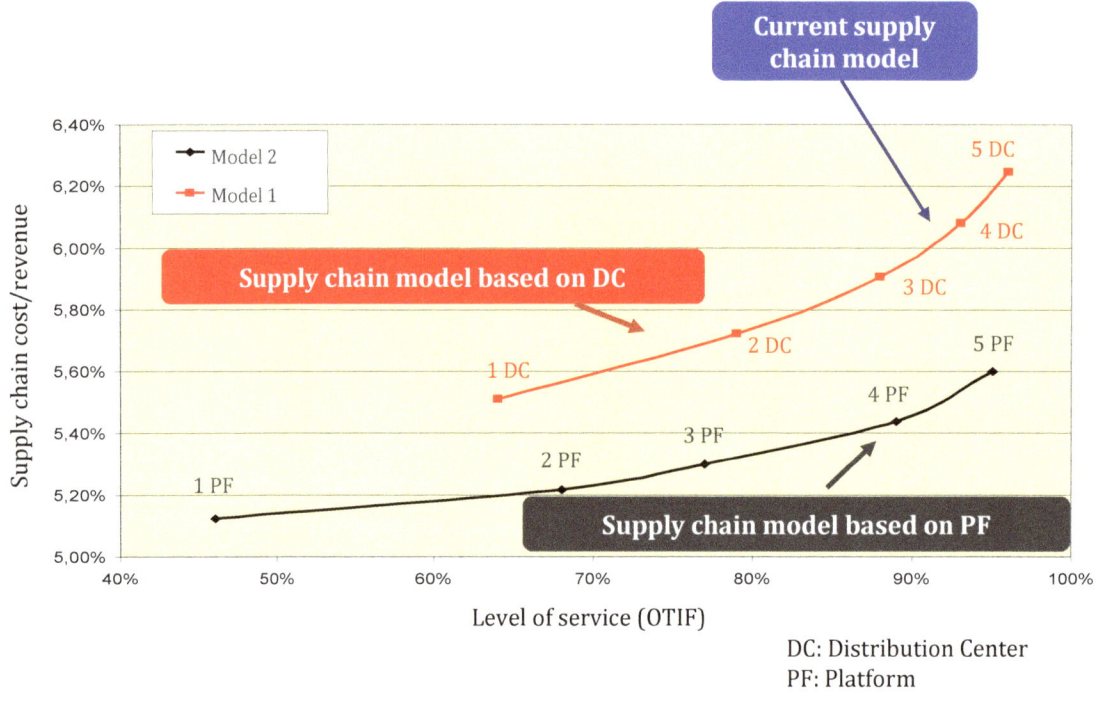

Diag.4: Disruption of an SC network

This is a disruptive evolution characterised by the withdrawal of the DC network, which means hundreds of thousands of m², the elimination of the local inventories, the development of logistics platforms probably subcontracted to a 3PL (third party logistics), the redesign of the transportation plan and the implementation of a new transportation management system to manage those new flows and new carriers within this new SC model.

## c) Digitalise your organisation

Digitalisation of the SC is probably the most disruptive transformation. Table 1 lists the most critical challenges a company faces through the digitalisation of its SC.

| Domains | Challenge |
|---|---|
| Customer needs | Understand how digital solutions can increase the WTP. |
| Suppliers and partners | Redefine the transaction way through interconnected and integrated solutions. |
| New offers | Educate the market to develop the acceptance of new offers and new channels based on digital solutions. |
| New way of working | Digital solutions enable us to boost mobile work, which is an opportunity for a higher flexibility and agility, but people have to be supported in adopting them. |
| Market entrance | Accelerate the time-to-market of new digital solutions. |
| Governance | Decision-making issues such as the fear of losing power. |
| Risk | Assess the risks related to the introduction of new digital solutions. |
| Finance | Difficulty to build up a business case for digital solutions selection and implementation. |
| Transparency | Fear of some stakeholders losing control of information due to a higher transparency of information. |
| Trust | Definition of confidentiality on exchanged data with suppliers and customers. |
| Data security | Fear of hacking, lack of confidentiality, reliability and data protection. |
| Roll-out management | Implementing a digital solution is not done through the same way as implementing a traditional information system. An appropriate iterative test and learn approach has to be followed and people in charge have to betrained in that purpose. |
| Obsolescence | Clear prioritisation of the most appropriate digital solutions has to be done in order to generate the highest value. |
| Competences and attitudes | People have to be trained for facing those new technologies and to be able to use the right language in terms of both competences and attitudes to get the positive benefits of such technologies. |
| Resistance to change | Manage the barriers to the established mindset, the need for flexibility and the redesign of processes and methods. |

Tab.1: Challenges of digitalisation (adapted from Prof. Dileep Kumar, Feb. 2020)

In Chapter 9 we have proposed a map of the digital solutions appropriate to SC with three main axes: connectivity, data analytics and smart automation. The IT solutions fulfil those axes by:

- Integrating the best of breeds of fragmented specialised IT modules (advanced planning systems, forecasting, production planning, transportation optimisation).
- Enabling quick decisions according to the last events from the demand or the supply side and simulating what-if scenarios coupling tactical and operational horizons.
- Routinising such analysis and decisions based on automated algorithms and hardware enabling close interaction between the people and the systems.

Such digitalisation enables us to:

- Drive the organisation by value in order not only to maximise the value generated by the current business model of the company but also to unlock new sources of performance and competitiveness. We will provide complementary insights in the next paragraph on that first axis of value creation by digitalisation.
- Foster transparency and collaboration between the stakeholders. Digitalisation without a higher integration and collaboration doesn't work. The commitment of all people to this new way of working is key.
- Develop a holistic approach based on cross-functional transparency along the end-to-end SC and on both bottom-up and top-down processes.
- Focus on performance and accountability of people to deliver the expected performance level.
- Reinforce the involvement of the external stakeholders within the SC model.

In order to make this disruption a success, organisations and people will have 'to unlearn what they know, to disrupt their habits and the existing power structures and to install disciplined business processes.' (Beath and al., 2019). An operational backbone has to be built up based on:

- Standardised collaborative processes enabling a seamless end-to-end SC.
- Shared data based on a single source: one set of numbers used for providing different levels of granularity according to the type of decisions to be made.
- Common applications to support agile processes synchronising the physical flows of goods with the information flows.
- Shared technologies reinforcing integration and collaboration, and enabling us to

build up a digital twin as a common asset for the company to support initiatives, analytics and simulation.
- Corporate networks and infrastructure services.

### d) Design a data model according to your strategic configuration

As mentioned in the previous paragraph, digitalisation enables us to explore new ways of value creation by unlocking unexplored areas of value. We have developed an approach based on the value model review and pointing out four types of companies in terms of their value model management according to their strategic configuration. The following diagram shows those four types:

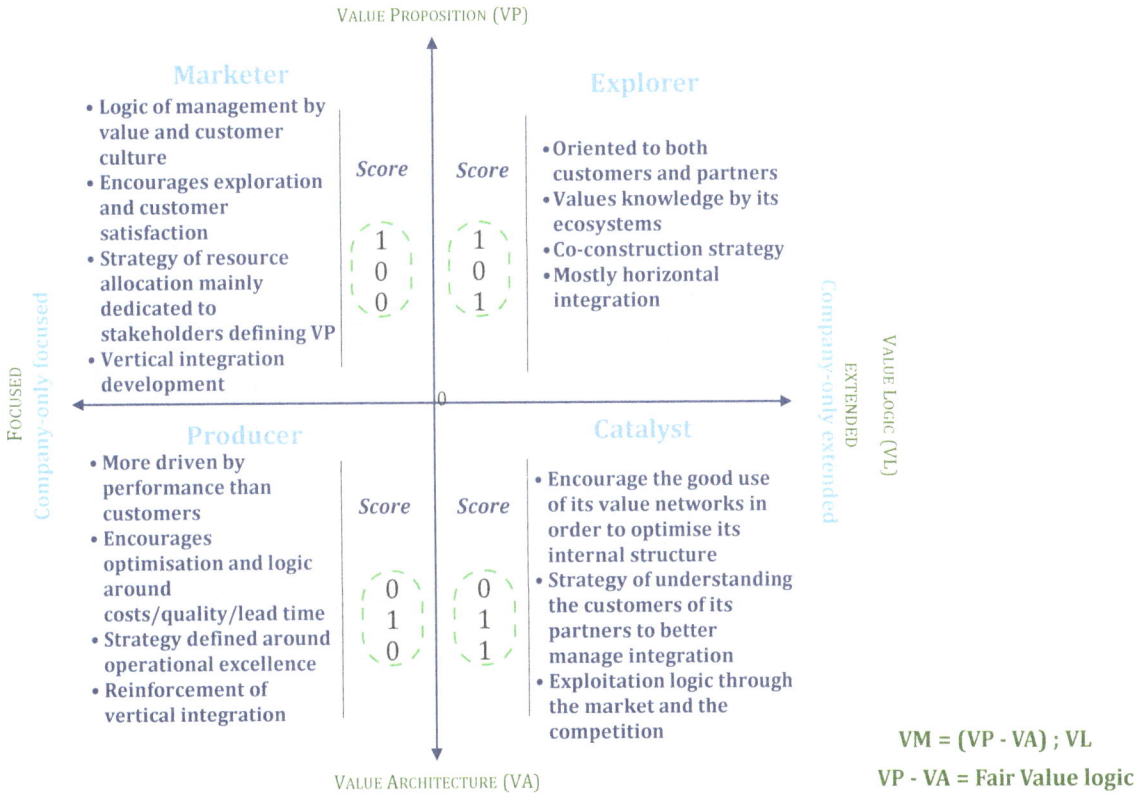

Diag.5: Value model review and strategic configurations (Alcaud & Fender, 2018)

The typology is based on the concept of business model (Osterwalder, 2010) completed by the notion of the logic value:

- The horizontal axis is linked to the value logic, which can be focused on internal operations or extended by involving the stakeholders of the company ecosystem.
- The vertical axis is represented by the value proposition versus the value architecture.

A research program run through a partnership between HEC Paris et Tallis Consulting (Alcaud & Fender, 2018) revealed four types of strategic configurations in terms of value model management:

- The **Producer** is a company with VP, VA, VL as (0,1,0) focused on internal players and the optimisation of the in-house operations. This type of company is driven by the optimisation and the operational performance according to the offer of products and services. Its objectives are structured around costs, quality and delivery lead-times in order to maximise the generated value by its products and services. Its value logic is the **rationalisation** of value.
- The **Marketer** (1,0,0) is driven by customer centricity and optimises its sales and marketing operations. The main objective of this company is to exploit the maximum potential of its products and services for revenue generation by getting the higher level of customer satisfaction. Its value logic is the **exploitation of the perceived value**.
- The **Explorer** (1,0,1) manages its value model by benefiting from its customers and partners to boost its value proposition. This type explores all opportunities of value creation from and to customers and partners. Its strategy is to continuously renew and improve its offers by being as much as possible connected to its customers. The logic value is value creation by **extending the offers** especially in services.
- The **Catalyst** (0,1,1) optimises its value architecture by benefiting from its customers and partners. This company is highly connected to the external ecosystem and increases its learning through its value networks in order to catch up the maximum value from those networks. Its value logic is learning by value and **monetising**.

In order to maximise the performance of a given business model, a balance between VP and VA generates an optimised VM (value management) but is not correlated to an extended value logic. The research pointed out the key role of SCM to support the vision of the general managers to have an optimised value model due to their focus of managing all operations by value. Programs of operational excellence (see the testimony of Saint-Gobain later in this chapter) are based on a strong integration of value proposition and value architecture and lead to a company transformation.

This typology model is dynamic. It means that according to the strategy of the company, there is a potential shift from a configuration type to another one. In that strategic move, we consider that the data model plays a key role as follows (Alcaud & Fender, 2020):

- As a Producer, with the objective to improve and automatise the back, middle and front office processes, the data model will support automated customer interface, predictive maintenance for the production facilities and predictive customer churn.
- As a Marketer, the link between WTP and the cost-to-serve enables to optimise the pricing and to monetise at the right level the offers. Data mining related to customer satisfaction and to competitors are key to support such strategic configuration.
- As an Explorer, the data model should detect opportunities of developing new revenue through valuing the data. Therefore, the company can extend its offer and test and learn new solutions.
- As a Catalyst, cooperation and competition are embedded in order to maximise the value learnt from the network partners. The data model will be designed in order to capture those data and the SC will play a key role to implement such data models.

The research program shows that if there is a core data model (common platform to any type of strategic configuration), each strategic configuration is characterised by a specific data model in terms of strategy (is data considered as a key asset?), governance (is there a governance dedicated to data?), infrastructures and tools (data access and accuracy), modelling (use of mathematical predictive models), utilisation and operation (quality, cleaning, management, update of data) and security and compliance (confidentiality).

Designing and implementing an appropriate data model specific to a strategic configuration is a disruptive transformation and points out the strategic role of data. The role of SCM is that transformation engaging value proposition, value architecture and value logic is clear.

Part B  Design and animate the right supply chain models to create a competitive advantage

## 3. Transform your organisation through an action plan

The action plan will integrate both incremental actions to exploit the existing business model and disruptive actions to generate new ways of value creation. On the following diagram, projects have been categorised according to the potential value creation and the project intensity in three clusters of actions to:

- Fix a pain point or a need such as automatising a SC dashboard.
- Improve an existing process or resource such as training people.
- Transform in-depth the business model at the value proposition and the value architecture levels such the implementation of IBP, the segmentation of SC models and the SC digitalisation.

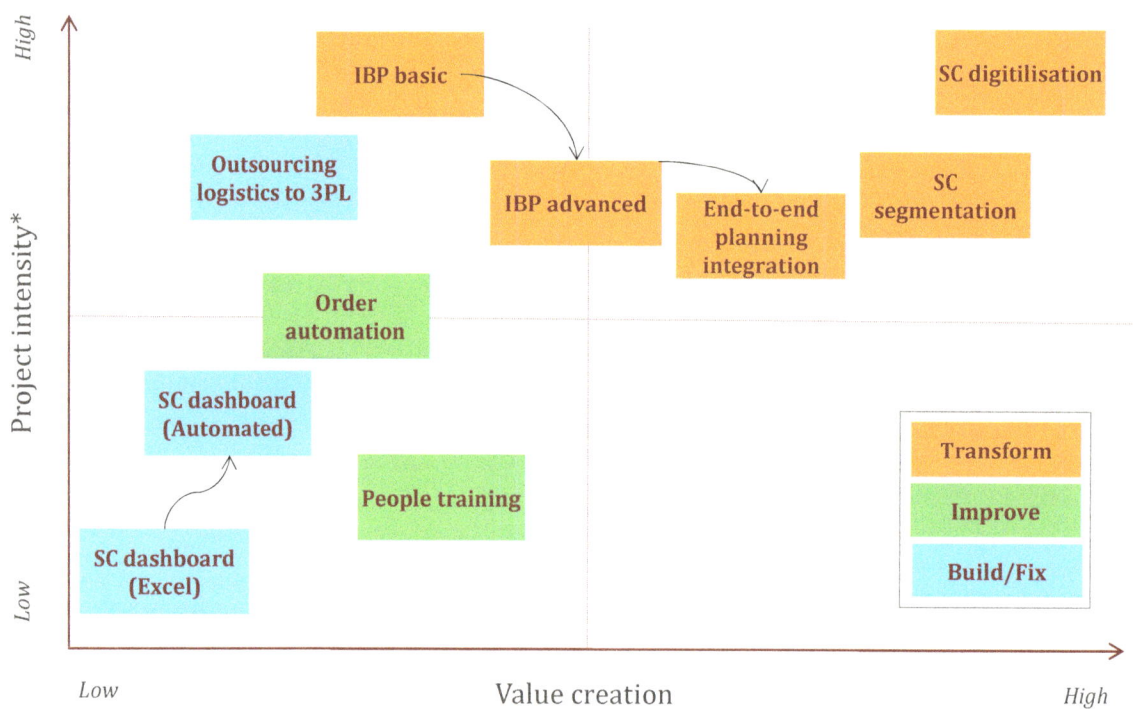

Diag.6: Mapping of the SC transformation projects

An SC transformation plan is a multi-dimensional and multi-year journey. We recommend appointing a steerco for following the progress, pointing out the issues and the resistance and the delays and to structure this plan around work packages categorised by the main building blocks, which are in the following example:

- Voice of customers for all projects related to the value proposition.
- Performance control including the SC dashboard, the reporting processes and the financial metrics.
- Planning covering the MTS/MTO selection, the decoupling point design and the S&OP implementation.
- Governance defining roles, missions and accountabilities.
- Digital tools and execution processes.
- Operational excellence in terms of logistics and people performance.

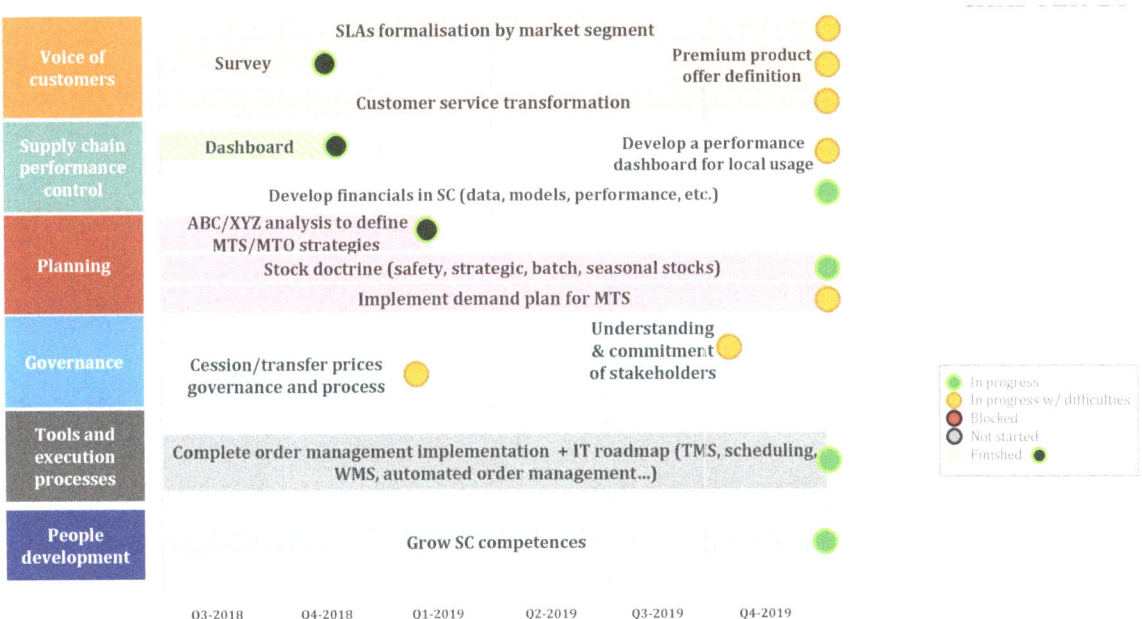

Diag.7: Work packages of an SC transformation plan

# Testimony from Saint-Gobain Gypsum and Insulation

Claude-Alain TARDY, CEO Gypsum and Insulation, Saint-Gobain (2014-2018), CEO Specialised Businesses (since 2018).

*Andreas BECK-ULM, Streamline Director Gypsum and Insulation, Saint-Gobain (2016-2018), Streamline Director Saint-Gobain (2019). Complementary comments from Mr Beck-Ulm in italic.*

### What are the main business challenges in your industry?

Our industry is very competitive and needs almost perfect execution, daily. We have to be excellent at delivering so-called commodities at competitive prices while permanently trying to differentiate ourselves with unique products delivering value to the final user.

When we launched Streamline we were well advanced in our world-class manufacturing program as well as our commercial efficiency program, without mentioning the already well-established financial and purchasing discipline embedded within the Saint-Gobain culture. I had however, each time I was visiting one of our 120 businesses throughout the world, the strange feeling that some kind of lubricant was missing in our organisations to make them really world class in terms of customer satisfaction.

### Could you explain the motivation to launch Streamline?

I initiated Streamline 5 years ago because I thought that a project around supply chain could become the missing lubricant I mentioned before. Thus I decided to launch this program with the goal to 'improve customer service while reducing working capital', purposely mentioning these two dimensions often mistakenly seen as antagonistic. My goal was to create interest in managing directors, not only customer service or supply chain managers.

*What is the content of this program and why this name?*

The name 'Streamline' was selected in order to position this project as a transversal one, aiming at chasing the inefficiencies throughout the organisation, in particular between functional players. *You will find the word 'team' embedded in Streamline, it is about collaboration – working together towards one common goal – and one set of numbers all departments align to work with and trust.*

*How has been this program been deployed at the worldwide level?*

Actually, this is more than a program, rolled out now in more than 50 business units. This is a transformational journey, which relies on a true cultural change based on a collective ownership and a shared leadership at the management team level in order to enable business decisions based on clear arbitrations. Beyond customer satisfaction and cash optimisation, building One Team at each business unit is definitely a take-away of that initiative.

*What is the role that supply chain management plays in its success?*

To implement this program I put together a small team made of experienced supply chain managers and young talents from different functions (marketing, finance, etc.) to lead this initiative and enrich it with each roll-out. They asked Michel Fender to put together a two-day training module aimed at preparing the management teams for achieving the expected value. *Local supply chain management takes the role to animate and facilitate the cross-functional processes with the full engagement and the fundamental shared leadership at management level.*

*What are the main outcomes and learnt lessons after 5 years of implementation?*

I must recognise that this project has delivered even more than I expected thanks to a great harmony between our internal consultants and Michel Fender. Michel has been instrumental in bringing the managing directors and their teams, in many very diverse cultures, to face the reality of our inefficiencies and fix them with a structured, long lasting approach based on common sense and teamwork. It has broken many internal silos and this project has become a resounding success story.

## Take-away for leaders

SCM has several credentials to support a transformational journey:

- SCM is the most cross-functional process at both internal and external levels. If you decide to change a part of your business model, SCM can play a critical role by facilitating and coordinating this change.

- SCM is a big consumer of data and a big provider of data as SCM connects all the stakeholders of the value chain. The digitalisation, that means a way to generate, manage, use, communicate, share and value data, is the most frequent driver of a transformation project.

- The success of a project relies on many parameters. One of them is the trust among the players and the commitment of them. The mission of SCM as explained previously is to develop trust, and therefore SCM being accountable to lead such transformation project can be perceived as a key success factor.

- Differentiating incremental change generating improvements of the existing business model from disruptive innovations transforming deeply a part or the whole business model of the company is a must. Therefore, the mechanist approach has to be counterbalanced by a test and learn organic approach.

## Key questions to address

1. Have you a dedicated organisation or identified people within your company to detect potential transformation ideas?
2. How have you organised the exploitation versus the exploration of your current business model?
3. What are the last projects you have launched in connection to the value proposition, to the value architecture and to the value logic?
4. What is the ratio of projects you have run in the value proposition versus in the operating system?
5. What is, in your opinion, your strategic configuration type (see diagram 5)? Do you consider it relevant or do you have a plan for a strategic move?
6. What are the main lessons of the past transformation projects you have run in your company? Failures, resistance and successes?
7. Have you formalised a data model? Have you identified a specific role of SCM to play in the date model design, implementation and animation?
8. How do you involve SC managers in your transformation project, whatever the main topic can be?
9. Have you formalised a business case for your projects in digitalisation?
10. Do you have projects without a digital dimension?

# Pre-conclusion: Apply SC mindset, concepts and tools to any type of organisation

The content of this book is based on manufacturing companies that design, produce and sell tangible goods. The purpose of this pre-conclusion is to open the huge field of application of SC to the services industry, which includes banking (retail, investment, wealth management), fintech, insurance, investment funds, software development, education, entertainment, NGOs and professional services firms (consulting, legal, etc.). The companies in those industries produce and sell intangible services to their customers. Telco, hospitality and healthcare (hospitals) deliver services too but manage tangible means and resources.

This pre-conclusion is mostly based on the exchange we have with our EMBA participants at HEC Paris and especially at the TRIUM Global Executive MBA (HEC-LSE-NYU). Most participants have positions in such pure service companies and are challenged for their final assignment to apply the SC concepts and tools to their own business environment. We have to say that the most original and innovative papers belong to this series of intangible service-based business.

The supply chain of service industry (Drzymalski, 2012) is characterised by:

- Intangibility.
- Production and consumption are simultaneous.
- Heterogeneity (in delivery of 'service' or 'product') due to human decision-making.
- Perishability (short life-span of service).
- Client-based relationships.
- High levels of customer contact, the customers being involved in the creation and the delivery of the service.

## 1. The five-parameter value equation

The following table describes the potential topics covered by the five parameters of the value equation:

| Parameters | Topics |
|---|---|
| Customer offer | The level of service of the main competitive advantage for service industry and the customer experience based on trust is key to increasing the WTP. The notion of excellence of service is equal to customer perception minus customer expectation.<br>Formalisation of service charters and service level agreements.<br>Improve service to the existing customer base.<br>Attract new customers through a portfolio of offers.<br>The main attributes of this value parameter are:<br>    Immediate reply in case of need.<br>    On-time delivery (for instance troubleshooting car solutions in 1 hour for an insurance company).Customised services and experience.<br>    Time-to-market for launching new services.Problem solving.<br>    Payment to customers (less than 5 days for insurance covering a damage).<br>    Claims management. |
| OPEX | Cost-to-serve is key to ensure an acceptable margin.<br>The labour cost is often the biggest part.<br>For instance, in one software company the cost breakdown is as follows: labour: 57%, customer service: 23%, servers: 10%, software subscriptions: 10%, and the last part covers facilities, internet connectivity and hardware leases. |
| Working capital | Generally, there is no inventory in the service industry but a pool of people can be considered as an inventory. We can even apply the SC model to HR activity if we consider the end-to-end SC covering the recruitment, the allocation of jobs, the mobility within the company, the development of talents and the exit. In this approach, a person (such as a software developer or a consultant) could be considered a raw material, who will be trained to develop their skills in terms of expertise and industry knowledge to meet a customer demand.<br>In the retail bank, the cash management is a topic of optimisation coupled with a security issue, not only in terms of the global level but also in terms of location of the cash inventories.<br>The receivables from the clients are a clear concern: order-to-cash management. |

| Parameters | Topics |
|---|---|
| Assets utilisation | Real estate is a big part. Shared office is a solution to optimise the workspace. Delocalisation to offshoring capabilities is another solution applied by many service companies to get the benefits of lower labour costs and cheaper facilities. A major concern is the ramp up and the capability to scale up the activities. The workspace may not be a significant expense in a profit formula but it can have a significant impact on employee satisfaction. ORE (Overall Resource Efficiency) can be applied as the OEE. |
| Sustainability | Forming a One Team is a fully shared topic with manufacturing company. Effective utilisation of globally available high-skilled labour; follow-the-sun model optimises utilisation across regions. Talent attraction and retention are concerns. Risk management and supply chain resilience. SC is a perfect way to educate people on the multi-dimensional characteristic of business and the criticality of trade-offs. People safety. Reduction of wastes. Green service supply chain. |

As for manufacturing companies, the priorities depend on the strategy of the company and its market positioning, but whatever this strategy is, SCM is a great leverage to boost the service culture within any type of organisation.

## 2. The five building block operating system

The five building blocks are also relevant, as listed in the following table:

| Building blocks | Topics |
|---|---|
| Governance and KPIs | Definition of accountability roles for revenue growth thanks to high NPS, customer experience, claims management, time-to-market, demand forecast accuracy, ORE, assets returns, etc. |
| Processes | The SC planning strategy based on a decoupling point can be applied, for instance, to the software development business: the first part is made to stock (MTS) on the new functionality of the platform for developing mass volume low margin standard solutions – i.e. trying to get ahead of what the clients want rather than letting them drive it. The second part of the supply chain follows the make-to-order (MTO) where they bring in their own consultants to customise application using the base platform in a collaborative mode.<br>S&OP/IBP can be applied in order to plan the demand and to match it with the planned available resources and to anticipate ramp up or ramp down. Matching the planned demand with the available projected resources and allocating the customers' orders to the production sites according to people competences and types of equipment.<br>Demand plan has to be differentiated for the project-driven business (probabilistic) versus the recurrent business (statistic). |
| People | Skills and attitudes development.<br>Specialisation versus multi-skilled people managed as a pool of human resources.<br>Time management. |
| Operations | Streamlining the end-to-end process. Automation, outsourcing, near versus offshoring solutions.<br>Optimisation of the 'production' facilities network at the global level.<br>Risk management and multi-sourcing strategy.<br>Lean operations. |
| Data and IT | One set of numbers.<br>Data compliance.<br>Digital continuity including connectivity (including CRM) and analytics.<br>Tracking and tracing of activities. |

It would be interesting to know why the professionals and the academics have not paid so far attention to the application of SC to the service industry. Lean management has been widely applied in service firms such banks. This is not the case for SCM. Actually, as we have seen, the application of SC to some manufacturing industries is still in progress and there is definitely a lack of awareness for service companies' leaders for the potential benefits SCM can provide in terms of value creation. A reason can be the higher margin and the fact such firms have not so far met big shutdowns of their end-to-end supply chains. After the Covid-19 crisis, the opportunity to build up SCM activities in service companies could happen.

# Testimony from Car .Software Organisation by Volkswagen

**Dr. Martin HOFMANN, CHRO Car. Software Organisation by Volkswagen (since 2020)**

Volkswagen is one of the biggest automobile manufacturers worldwide. As a result, the employees of the company have a lot of opportunities to work in different positions, in different brands and in different countries. I started my career at Volkswagen with an internship in production and afterwards I wrote my thesis with a focus on corporate culture, which brought me later into the human resources team. There, I took over my first fulltime job in a department, which developed management policies and processes while working on my doctoral degree in parallel. The next opportunity took me on a 5 year assignment to China ramping up two transmission plants from scratch. As head of human resources and HR strategy I was part of the journey to go public with the Truck and Bus Group from Volkswagen, called TRATON, before I finally took over my current position as CHRO at Volkswagen's Software Organisation.

During the different steps of my career at Volkswagen, I had the opportunity to work on different challenges. But all challenges had one thing in common: the customer. Whether it was the top management or the blue-collar employees in the factory, the customer was always in focus. My first contact to SCM outside the classic logistic thinking happened during my MBA. It was eye opening to pivot the principle of SCM to different types of organisations and create a new context and opportunities to rethink processes. In particular, I found it interesting to apply this concept to the area of people and talent development within the human resource field.

The focus of SCM is to understand the customer and put them first. For all employees in the human resource business the most ambitious goal is to make their customer satisfied, while sticking to the organisational rules and applying lean and efficient processes. The human factor in this context makes it even more difficult to achieve this goal, as there is always a natural imbalance between customer expectations from the employee side and the provided solution from the company side. Let's take a deep dive into people and talent development. What happens if organisations would start from the customer end to rethink this topic? The learning interests of employees would drive people development, seminars and trainings based on a customer-centric learning journey. That means that the learning type, the training mode, and the preferred learning way would be centred on or even co-created based on individual needs. Here we have the connection to SCM. The continuous development need and the enhancement of competences to maintain employability based on individual strengths and preferences would change the way people are learning in organisations. Typical processes, where the leaders and managers decide which training is the best to cover their employees' needs, has to be reconsidered and consequently adjusted. A new way of thinking is necessary to facilitate the change, moving away from the classical training catalogue approaches. We have to think differently.

As a conclusion, we can see that there is a new way of learning when applying this SCM concept to traditional employee development. There is a need to seize this chance to motivate learners and create an individual employee learning experience. Only then will it enable the industries of the future to master their transformation through strong competency development.

# Conclusion

The ambition of this book is to convince business leaders to consider supply chain management as a critical or even strategic business topic. In terms of business leader mindset, the key perspective is to shift from avoiding supply chain breakdowns and negative impacts, especially on customers, to a proactive approach creating a sustainable value as a competitive advantage. After the Covid-19 crisis, this is time to move from a single efficiency focus to a more sophisticated SCM value roadmap based on agility, resilience, sustainability, responsibility and innovation. Less advanced companies consider SC as an internal support activity, whereas the more advanced appreciate it as a support service to the customers, and the top ones as an activity generating value to the consumers. We hope we have contributed to changing your mindset on that business opportunity, whatever your business is.

Let's conclude on the main reasons that could motivate you to give to supply chain management such a role and to design a next generation supply chain:

- SCM, by monitoring both tactical and operational activities, is the perfect process to **link your strategy to its operational execution**. SCM is the complementary leverage beyond the strategy design to implement it.
- SCM enables you to challenge the value proposition of your business model by formalising its **value equation** and its priorities in terms of value creation. SCM forces the managing team to formalize clear and shared **trade-off** rules.
- The SC operating system embeds all solutions including the digital ones, which provide a huge potential of value creation. The **fair value** paradigm enables you to make the right valuable choice of those solutions to properly serve your value equation and to avoid any value destruction related to your business model.
- By **streamlining** the organisations, developing **seamless** processes and **connecting** the stakeholders of a given business ecosystem, SCM enables you to detect opportunities and risks.
- Through S&OP/IBP, SCM enables the business to be more **agile**, to get benefits of business opportunities and to align the management team around a common value roadmap.
- Through simulating SC models, scenarios of multiple risks can be tested to detect vulnerabilities and opportunities and more **resilience** to face risks, whatever the type of risk is, can be increased.

## Conclusion

- Especially through **digitalisation**, SCM is a leverage of the company transformation by focusing on both **exploitation** and **exploration**.

Finally, beyond processes, automation and digital solutions, getting a higher value from SCM relies fundamentally on **talents** and a **united team,** animated by a true cooperation mindset. Through building **trust** between stakeholders, SCM is definitely a booster of the **collective intelligence**, which is a key success factor of our new normal life.

# Glossary

| | |
|---|---|
| APS | Advanced Planning Systems |
| DC | Distribution centre |
| E2E | End-to-End |
| EOQ | Economic Order Quantity |
| FCF | Free Cash Flow |
| IBP | Integrated Business Planning |
| IoT | Internet of Things |
| IS | Information System |
| IT | Information Technology |
| mOQ | Minimum Order Quantity |
| MOQ | Maximum Order Quantity |
| MRP | Manufacturing Resources Planning |
| MTO | Make-to-Order |
| MTS | Make-to-Stock |
| NPS | Net Promoter Score |
| OEE | Overall Equipment Efficiency |
| OSA | On Shelf Availability |
| OTIF | On Time In Full |
| POS | Point of Sales |
| PSA | Production Schedule Adherence |
| RTM | Route to Market |
| SC | Supply Chain |
| SCM | Supply Chain Management |
| SKU | Stock Keeping Unit |
| SLA | Service Level Agreement |
| SLOB | Slow Movers Obsolete |
| S&OE | Sales & Operations Execution |
| S&OP | Sales & Operations Planning |
| TMS | Transportation Management System |
| VMI | Vendor Managed Inventory |
| WACC | Weighted Average Cost of Capital |
| WCM | World Class Manufacturing |
| WMS | Warehouse Management System |

# Bibliography

Alcaud D., Fender M., Tixier JC. (2018), *Revue du modèle de valeur. Management par la valeur: un levier d'innovation et de performance*, Working Paper, Paris

Alcaud D., Fender M., Tixier JC. (2020), *Modèles d'exploitation de la donnée et stratégie d'entreprise*, Working Paper, Paris

Alexander M., Jaakkola E. (2015), 'Customer Engagement Behaviours and Value Co-creation', *Customer Engagement: Contemporary Issues and Challenges*, Chapter 1, p. 3-20

Alicke K., Bariball E., Lund S., Swan D (2020 May 14), *Is your supply chain risk blind or risk resilient?* McKinsey & Company.

Almquist E., Senior J., Bloch N. (2016), *The elements of value*, HBR

Amit R., Zott C. (July 2010), 'Business model innovation: creating value in times of change', IESE Business School

Beath C., Ross J., Mocker M. (2019), *Designed for Digital: How to Architect Your Business for Sustained Success*, MIT Press

de Boer R., van Bergen M., Steeman M. (2015), *Supply Chain Finance, its Practical Relevance and Strategic Value*, Windesheim University of Applied Sciences, second ed., www.scfcommunity.org

Blowers M., Petrie A., Holcomb M. (2017), *Unleashing the potential of supply chain analytics*, MIT Sloan Management Review.

Chenneveau D., Eloot K., Kuentz J.-F., Lehnich M. (2020), *Coronavirus and technology supply chains: How to restart and rebuild*, McKinsey & Company.

Drzymalski J. (2012), *Supply Chain Frameworks for the Service Industry: A Review of the Literature*, European International Journal of Science and Technology Vol. 1

Gereffi G. Humphrey J., Sturgeon T. (2005), « *The Governance of global value chains* », Review of International Political Economy, vol. 12, n°1, p.78-104

Griffin, D. (2018, August 16). *Supply Chain Management In The Service Industry*, from https://griffinandco.marketing/blog/2018/8/16/supply-chain-management-in-the-service-industry

Holweg M., Helo P. (2014), *Defining value chain architectures: linking strategies to operational supply chain design*. International Journal Production Economics.

Kim M., Raghuvanshi K., Bucciarelli R., Sodhi V. (2013 ). *Optimising the retail bank supply chain: How retail banks can lower costs, reduce inventory and boost productivity: Lessons from consumer business.* Deloitte

PP Klaus, S Maklan, (2013) « *Towards a Better Measure of Customer Experience: Explanatory Power and Generalisability* », International, Journal of Market Research

Lehman-Ortega L., Leroy F., Garette B., Dussauge P., Durand R. (2019), *Strategor*, Dunod, 8ème édition

Maretl A., Klibi W. (2016), *Designing Value-Creating Supply Chain Networks*, Springer

McKinsey Global Institute (August 2020), *Risk resilience and rebalancing in global value chains.*

Min H. (2019), *Blockchain technology for enhancing supply chain resilience*, Business Horizons.

Osterwalder A., Pigneur Y. (2010), *Business Model Generation: A Handbook for Visionaries, Game Changers, and Challengers*, John Wiley & Sons.

Osterwalder A., Pigneur Y., Tucci C. (June 2010), « *Clarifying Business Models : Origins, Present and Future of the Concept* », Actes de l'Association for Information Systems, vol.15, p. 751-775.

Otto, B. (2011, June). *A morphology of the organisation of data governance.* ECIS, vol. 20, No. 1, p. 1.

Pascal, M.V. (2016) *How to Apply Supply Chain Management to The Financial Services Industry.* Retrieved from https://www.linkedin.com/pulse/how-apply-supply-chainmanagement-financial-services-pascal.

Perez H. (2013), *Supply chain strategies: which one hits the mark?* CSCMP's Supply Chain Quaterly.

Priem R. L., Tantalo C. (2014), *'Value creation through stakeholder synergy'*, Strategic Management Journal

Rezgui, Y. (2007), *Knowledge systems and value creation: An action research investigation*, Industrial Management & Data Systems, Vol. 107 No. 2, pp. 166-182.

Sakhuja,S., Jain, V. (2012) *Service supply Chain : An Integrated conceptual Framework*, Indian Institute of Technology.

Sheng J., Amankwah-Amoah J., Wang X., (2017) *A multidisciplinary perspective of big data in management research*, International Journal of Production Economics, Volume 191, pages 97-112.

Shih W. (2020, March 19), *Is it time to rethink globalised supply chains?* MIT Sloan Management Review.

Treacy M., Wiersema F. (1993), *Customer intimacy and Other Value Disciplines*, HBR

Treacy M., Wiersema F. (1995) *The Discipline of Market Leaders*, Perseus Book

www.ingramcontent.com/pod-product-compliance
Ingram Content Group UK Ltd.
Pitfield, Milton Keynes, MK11 3LW, UK
UKHW062045180426
11947UKWH00030B/2048